Helion & Company Limited
Unit 8 Amherst Business Centre
Budbrooke Road
Warwick
CV34 5WE
England
Tel. 01926 499 619
Email: info@helion.co.uk
Website: www.helion.co.uk
Twitter: @helionbooks
Visit our blog http://blog.helion.co.uk/

Text © Edward Crowther 2022
Photographs © as individually credited
Colour figures Giorgio Albertini © Helion &
    Company 2022; colour profiles by and ©
    David Bocquelet 2022
Maps: Tiago Alexandre Batista © Helion &
    Company 2022

Designed and typeset by Farr out
    Publications, Wokingham, Berkshire
Cover design Paul Hewitt, Battlefield Design
    (www.battlefield-design.co.uk)

ISBN 978-1-915070-66-1

British Library Cataloguing-in-Publication
    Data
A catalogue record for this book is available
    from the British Library

We always welcome receiving book
proposals from prospective authors.

CONTENTS

MAP OF EUROPE SINCE 1992

Note: In order to simplify the use of this book, all names, locations and geographic designations are as provided in *The Times World Atlas*, or other traditionally accepted major sources of reference, as of the time of described events.

INTRODUCTION AND ACKNOWLEDGEMENTS

This book is about the armed formations of the Donetsk People's Republic (DPR), a de facto political entity in eastern Ukraine, covering the period in time from their creation in 2014 to their official recognition by the Russian Federation in February 2022.

The armed formations of the DPR were widely acknowledged to be the more powerful and combat effective of the two unrecognised de facto entities in eastern Ukraine, the other being that of the neighbouring Luhansk People's Republic (LPR). A better understanding of the armed formations of the DPR, and its role as a key proxy force for the Kremlin, improves understanding of the Ukraine conflict.

This book seeks to bring the armed formations of the DPR during this period into greater focus, explaining the history of their creation, motivational ideology, structure, capabilities and equipment. In total, the armed formations of the DPR and LPR together are thought to have numbered some 40,000 people, but in the West they were often glossed over in a single line as 'separatist' or 'pro-Russian' forces.

The relationship of the DPR with its patron state, the Russian Federation, will also be examined. To utilise the terminology of the study of proxy warfare, the complex and changing nature of the relationship between the 'benefactor' (Russia) and the 'proxy' (the DPR) will be explored.[1]

Simply put, the DPR as a Kremlin proxy developed – as most proxies do – its own internal dynamics, and interests that ran parallel and sometimes counter to those of the Kremlin. This is not to absolve the Kremlin of responsibility in sparking and then fanning the flames of conflict in Donbas, thereby turning hitherto mostly peaceful political differences into an armed conflict that had – by the end of 2021 – already claimed around 14,000 lives.

Rather, this book is an attempt to aid external comprehension of the DPR and its armed formations as de facto entities, but to be clear, understanding does not imply justification. To borrow the words of the geographer Gerard Toal about the invasions of Georgia and Ukraine: 'Understanding is not justification. Given the high stakes involved … it is vital that we strive to deeply comprehend Russia's invasions of 2008 and 2014.'[2]

This book will take it as axiomatic that the DPR's armed formations were heavily supplied and supported by the Russian Federation, and that the DPR was almost entirely reliant on Russian political, military and financial support. More fundamentally, the Kremlin acted from 2014 to early 2022 as the sole 'security guarantor' for the two People's Republics in eastern Ukraine.

By employing proxy forces in Donbas, the Kremlin sought to lower international accountability for the ensuing violence by building in degrees of separation from the Russian state. This separation was not without cost though, as there were serious problems of delegation, command and control – manifested in the often unruly, chaotic and violent nature of the DPR's armed formations and indeed the DPR more broadly.[3]

The DPR was chaotic and unstable from the moment of its creation and formed – along with the neighbouring LPR – an area in eastern Ukraine where people lived outside the norms of international rule of law, suffering an extreme drop in living standards and freedom of movement. This book does not wish to glamourise the DPR's armed formations, who as well as fighting the Ukrainian state, ensured control for the DPR's rulers, despite the well-rehearsed trappings of imitation democracy.

As this book was being finalised in early 2022, the relatively static or 'frozen' nature of the conflict in eastern Ukraine was altered, first by the official recognition of the DPR and LPR as independent states by the Russian Federation on 21 February 2022, and then by the massive Russian 'special military operation' into Ukraine that commenced on 24 February 2022.

In a speech on 24 February, one of Putin's stated goals for the 'special military operation' was to come to the aid of the Donetsk and Luhansk People's Republics, and he referred to treaties of 'friendship and mutual assistance' that had been ratified just two days earlier.[4]

'Defenders of Donbass.' Magnet, c. 2016. The outline of the Donetsk People's Republic on the left depicts the whole of pre-conflict Donetsk oblast, only around 30 percent of which was controlled by the DPR at the time. (Author's collection)

A constellation of just some of the DPR and LPR armed formation units that were unleashed in eastern Ukraine. Among the insignia of various DPR 1st Army Corps units which will be discussed in this book are the insignia for the LPR's Prizrak (Призрак, Russian for 'ghost') unit, and a morale patch for 'Sofa warriors' (Диванные войска). Magnet, c. 2016. (Author's collection)

The outcome of this 'special military operation' was, at the time of writing, still to be determined. DPR 1st Army Corps units were heavily engaged in the fighting, and involved in advances towards the urban centres of Volnovakha and Mariupol. What is clear is that the outcome of the Kremlin's 'special military operation', one way or other, will determine the future of the DPR and LPR as political entities.

This book was always meant to be historical rather than predictive in its formulation, and will outline the turbulent creation and often chaotic nature of the armed formations of the DPR from 2014 to February 2022 when these formations joined Putin's 'special military operation.' These DPR formations are now involved – fighting alongside the forces of the Russian Federation – in the massive conflict in eastern Ukraine, the outcome of which will reshape the security architecture of Europe.

Scope of Focus

By focusing on the DPR's armed formations, the role of Russian Federation regular units, in particular in the first two years of conflict, will be discussed where relevant, but in terms of a necessary limitation of scope this book will not examine these units in great detail. Similarly, the much-publicised role of the Russian Private Military Company (PMC) Wagner Group, in particular at Debaltseve, will be touched upon, but similarly this PMC and its use by Russia in Donbas is not the book's primary focus.

Methodology

This book was written entirely from open-source information, utilising sources in the Ukrainian, Russian and English languages.

It aims to collect and synthesise these various information sources and provide a concise and readable account of the DPR's armed formations, in particular for the reader who may be less familiar with some of the disparate information sources available on the conflict in eastern Ukraine.

One major feature of the conflict in eastern Ukraine from 2014 to 2022 was the intense use of information warfare of all kinds. From a position of relative military weakness, compared to the Ukrainian state, as well for reasons of bombast and 'nation building' propaganda, the DPR had a strong incentive to continuously exaggerate its military capabilities in its official media. For this reason, official reports or media products produced by the DPR during this period should be treated with caution.

A second major source of information was Ukrainian or Western open-source investigation and reporting into the DPR's capabilities. Ukrainian open-source investigation was usually incredibly detailed, and often written with the benefit of a deep understanding of the terrain and actors involved. However, for various understandable reasons, which will be discussed in more depth below, Ukrainian sources tended to place a much greater emphasis on the role of the Russian Federation in the DPR's armed formations, often denying any form of 'agency' on the part of the DPR at all.

The book therefore attempts to synthesise various sources of information about the DPR's armed formations and present them in what it hopes will be a balanced way.

Terms, Naming Conventions and Transliteration

Any writing about the DPR and the Ukraine conflict has to take a position on terminology.

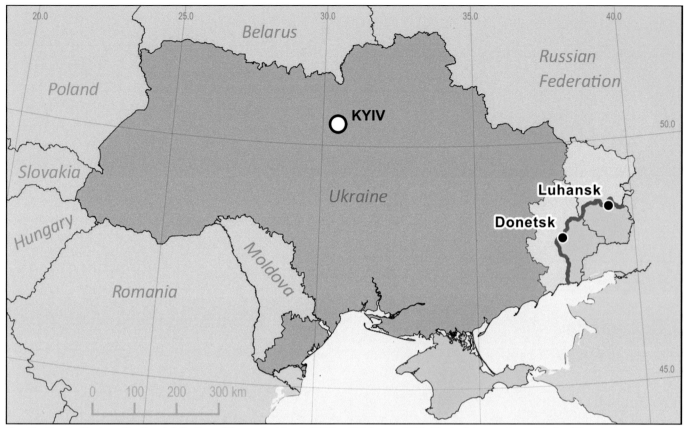

The situation in Ukraine, after the stabilisation of the contact line in 2015 until February 2022. Ukraine's two eastern oblasts of Donetsk and Luhansk are indicated (other oblasts in Ukraine are not shown for clarity). The red line is the contact line, to the east of which were the two Non-Government-Controlled Areas occupied by the DPR and LPR. The Crimean Peninsula, occupied from 2014 onwards by the Russian Federation, is similarly indicated. (Map by Tiago Alexandre Batista)

Definition of Areas

This is a book primarily about the armed formations of the DPR, which was for the period of focus of the book the de facto entity in control of a significant part of Donetsk oblast in eastern Ukraine. However, defining what the DPR was as an entity is challenging in itself.

Those areas in eastern Ukraine not under the control of the Ukrainian state were called different things, generally dependent on political persuasion. Some authors and international organisations favoured 'Non-Government-Controlled Areas' (NGCA) or 'Certain Areas of Donetsk Oblast' (CADO), whereas in government-controlled Ukraine the term 'Occupied Regions of Donetsk and Luhansk Oblasts' (ORDiLO) was also often used.[5]

Since around mid-2015, when the initially highly fluid contact line solidified into a static front line which barely changed until February 2022, around 7,850 square kilometres of Donetsk oblast[6] were estimated to be under the control of the DPR. This area amounted to 30 percent of the oblast's pre-conflict area, though this area contained many of the oblast's key cities such as Donetsk, and major industrial cities such as Horlivka.

Lacking formal international recognition even from their patron state, the Russian Federation, the DPR existed from 2014 as a de facto entity of uncertain status in the territorial area of eastern Ukraine. The best definition for the DPR is probably that of an 'unrecognised state', following the work of the academic Nina Caspersen on such entities. She suggests that an unrecognised state must meet the following criteria: '1) The entity has achieved de facto independence. 2) Its leadership is seeking to build further state institutions and demonstrate its own legitimacy. 3) The entity has sought, but not achieved, international recognition. 4) It has existed for at least 2 years.'[7]

However, de facto independence did not equate to automatic demands for statehood, and as one Ukrainian academic noted in 2018, '…there is no complete picture of whether today's Luhansk and Donetsk 'republics' are states or, if not, what their administrative and territorial status really is … So, in the Donetsk 'republic's' schools, the region is studied as part of courses concerning geographical matters, and in the curriculums and textbooks of these courses the Donbas is merely called an "area" (край).'[8]

Definition of Organisations

As with many other unrecognised states around the world, from 2014 the DPR quickly launched into building state-like institutions, usually mimicking those of its patron state, the Russian Federation.

It was understandably common in pro-Ukrainian circles to refer to such institutions in apostrophes, in order to reject their legitimacy, or similarly to prefix the titles of ministers or other functionaries of the DPR with words such as 'so-called' or 'self-proclaimed' for a similar reason. Under Ukrainian law, the DPR and its armed formations were quickly classified as terrorist organisations.

For the purposes of clarity, this book will refer to DPR ministries, organisations, and the people in charge of them as they would refer to themselves. This is to aid comprehension and clarity, and does not imply acceptance or confer legitimacy.

Place Names

In 2015, Ukraine enacted a series of laws on decommunization, which aimed to remove references to the country's Soviet past. As a result, thousands of streets, villages, towns and cities were renamed, and Communist-era statues and memorials removed.

For the DPR and LPR, a rejection of this attempt to erase the Soviet past became one of the most visual differences between

A bust of Lenin at one of the DPR-controlled entry-exit checkpoints by which civilians entered and left the DPR. April 2018. (Private photo collection, used with permission)

Ukraine and the two non-government-controlled areas in Donbas. As statues of Lenin were taken down across the rest of Ukraine –

one in Odesa was famously turned into a memorial to Darth Vader[9] – they remained standing in the DPR and LPR-controlled cities of Donetsk, Luhansk, Ilovaisk, Alchevsk, and many others.

As a side note, many commonly used international mapping websites and softwares had by 2022 yet to change many places to the new official names.

As this book refers to places within the territory of Ukraine, and for consistency, it will utilise those place names officially designated by the Ukrainian state, though in places may also sometimes append the former place name in addition to aid comprehension. Similarly, the anglicised variants of Ukrainian place names will be utilised, such as 'Donbas' rather than 'Donbass'.[10] Where someone else is being quoted, the spelling in the original text will be retained.

Linguistic Note

The Donetsk People's Republic (DPR) is sometimes found referred to in some English language material as DNR, this stems from a direct transliteration of the DPR's acronym in Russian: Donetskaya Narodnaya Respublika.

Elsewhere, there may be small differences in the spelling of certain people's names, owing to differing transliterations from Russian. The book attempts to maintain consistency in its own spellings throughout but retains the spellings of people's names in quotations as per the original.

Acknowledgements

Many people contributed to the completion of this book. To those friends who contributed photos to be used for this book, the author extends his gratitude. Others spent summer and winter days at markets and in shopping centres to collect some of the physical material displayed here. Special thanks go to Tiago Alexandre Batista for the maps, and to Tom Cooper at Helion for the patient understanding and constant support.

1

ORIGINS OF THE CONFLICT IN EASTERN UKRAINE

In order to understand the armed formations of the DPR, and indeed more broadly the DPR itself as a de facto political entity, it is necessary to briefly examine the origins of the conflict in eastern Ukraine, and situate it within a broader background of increased geostrategic conflict between Russia and the West.

Effectively, the causes of the conflict in eastern Ukraine have their origins in both international geostrategic conflict, and internal divisions within Ukraine that have deep-seated historical roots. As the scholar Serhy Yekelchyk notes: 'The fighting in ... Donetsk and Luhansk provinces combines features of a covert foreign invasion with those of a civil conflict. Accordingly, it has both external and internal causes, even if these happen to be closely connected.'[1]

Geostrategic Background

The increasing geostrategic competition between the West and Russia is complex in origin but can be traced to dynamics that emerged in the wake of the collapse of the Soviet Union. Though the breakup of the Soviet Union was largely peaceful, Russia found itself bordered by newly-independent former Soviet republics, as well as

former Warsaw Pact states in Eastern Europe. The academic Paul D'Anieri notes that the '...end of the Cold War set in motion two forces that were necessarily in tension: democratization in eastern Europe and Russia's insistence that it retain its "great power" status [...] Ukraine was the place where democracy and independence most challenged Russia's conception of its national interests.'[2]

Over the course of the 1990s and 2000s, the two major Euro-Atlantic organisations, NATO and the European Union, welcomed to their ranks newly democratic, former Warsaw Pact countries like Poland, Hungary and Romania, as well as former Soviet republics like Estonia, Latvia and Lithuania. Russia saw this expansion as both a threat to its security, and an unwelcome intrusion into areas it considered within its sphere of influence.

The NATO campaign in Yugoslavia in the late 1990s, and the 2003 invasion of Iraq, further soured the relationship between Russia and the West. In the minds of Russian strategic thinkers, the West was willing to act unilaterally when it suited Western, and primarily American, interests. The invasion of Iraq particularly rankled, as it occurred in the face of vocal Russian opposition and came only a few years after Russia had provided what it saw as enthusiastic support for the US-led Global War on Terror after 2001.

In May 2008, at the NATO summit in Bucharest, NATO offered a promise of possible membership to both Georgia and Ukraine. Though neither aspiring country was offered a Membership Action Plan, the beginning of the formal road to NATO membership, they were offered a promise that their applications for Membership Action Plans would be reviewed in December that same year.[3]

Russian President Vladimir Putin gave a speech to the media at the end of the Bucharest summit, in which he stated that further expansion of NATO, bringing it to Russia's borders, 'would be taken in Russia as a direct threat to the security of our country.'[4] Furthermore, increasing references were made in Russia to the supposed promise given at the end of the Cold War that NATO would not extend its membership eastwards.

After the summit, the diplomatic relationship between Russia and Georgia deteriorated rapidly, culminating in the brief, violent war between Russia and Georgia in August 2008.

Dynamics within Ukraine
Though an in-depth discussion of the history and politics of Ukraine would far exceed the remit of this book, with respect to understanding the DPR's armed formations it is important to briefly touch upon these to seek the origins of the DPR as a concept and entity.

There is a tendency, in particular in journalistic shorthand, to describe Ukraine as being divided into western Ukraine, seen as more pro-Western, and eastern Ukraine which is seen as more pro-Russian. Some commentators on Ukraine went as far as to equate 'Russian-speaking' as being tantamount to 'pro-Russian' in political leanings.

Very broadly summarised, the differences in language and culture within Ukraine stem from historical periods and processes which affected the various regions in diverging ways. Parts of western Ukraine were part of the Austro-Hungarian Empire well into the twentieth century, whereas eastern Ukraine was under Russian and then Soviet rule.

The area controlled by the DPR in 2019, as well as principle settlements, with the contact line marked in red. To the northeast, across the oblast border and east of the contact line, is the territory of Ukraine that was controlled at the time by the LPR. (Map by Tiago Alexandre Batista)

In eastern Ukraine, and the Donbas in particular, heavy industrialisation and cultural 'Russification' were promoted by first the Russian Empire and the Soviets that followed. In western Ukraine, the Austro-Hungarian Empire discouraged industrialisation, while also allowing the teaching of the Ukrainian language. Parts of what are now western Ukraine did finally come under Soviet rule at the end of the Polish-Soviet War in 1921 and the partition of Poland in the Second World War, but consequently spent less time under Soviet rule until the collapse of the Soviet Union in 1991.

The academics Menon and Rumer neatly summarise this, noting that '…the divergent experiences of western Ukrainians and their kin in the south and east have left their mark … in the form of differences on matters ranging from identity and internal politics to foreign policy. These differences would re-emerge in 2013 – 2014 and segue into a clash between Russia and the West over Ukraine's future.'[5]

Early DPR propaganda mixed both celebration of the region's industrial self-image with motifs of armed resistance – here a coal miner wearing a mining helmet shoulders a Kalashnikov. Magnet, c. 2016. (Author's collection)

Politically, and with similar broad summarisation, following independence in 1991 Ukraine had a series of presidents who tried to tread different paths between the West and Russia. In 2014, the president was Viktor Yanukovych, against whom the Euro Maidan protests of 2013-14 erupted in Kyiv. These protests, and the outcome of them, will be discussed in more detail below.

Donbas Region

The Donbas – its name a portmanteau of the words Donets River Basin – was a hitherto remote and underdeveloped part of the Russian Empire, dominated by the open and sparsely populated steppe. The industrialisation of the Donbas region began in the period of the Russian Empire, when concessions were opened to foreign concerns to import industrial technologies and begin heavy industrial enterprises in certain regions of the empire.

The catalyst for this development was, in part, Russia's defeat in the Crimean War, where the more technologically advanced Ottoman, British and French forces had been able to move more rapidly by sea, spurring a Russian desire for an improved internal railway network.

One of the regions which was earmarked for this rapid industrial development was the Donbas. Small deposits of coal had been worked there previously, but the Imperial Russian government realised they needed foreign expertise and investment to fully develop these resources.

A Welsh engineer, John Hughes, founded the city that would become Donetsk in 1869, and it began to grow rapidly. Nearby Luhansk was founded by a Scottish engineer, while Belgian industrial concerns developed what is now the Ukrainian city of Kostiantynivka in Donetsk oblast.

Rich coal deposits were soon linked by rail to iron ore deposits found at Kriviy Rih, and the resulting boom in metallurgical production attracted workers from across the Russian Empire and abroad, creating a multi-ethnic society with Russian as the standard *lingua franca*. Donetsk – then called Yuzovka after its Welsh founder – grew rapidly, along with the social problems that went hand-in-hand with nineteenth century industrialisation. Critically, the industrial cities and societies that attracted Russian-speaking workers from across the Russian Empire were culturally distinct from the Ukrainian agrarian society around them.

By 1917, when all foreign enterprises were nationalised by the Soviets after the October Revolution, the Donbas was one of the key industrial regions in the Soviet Union owing to its heavy industrial production. Moreover, the Soviet predilection for heavy industries, and favoured treatment and glorification of workers in such industries, also predisposed the population towards involvement in the greater Soviet project: 'The Soviet leadership celebrated the Donbas as the showcase of socialism, referring to the industrial achievements and the hard work performed by miners and heavy industrial workers.'[6]

By the 1970s however, the economy of the Donbas was stagnating, both as a result of the broader 'Brezhnev stagnation' across the Soviet Union, and the fact that many of the coal deposits had been worked out. The Donbas miners were instrumental in precipitating the collapse of the Soviet Union, after a series of strikes in 1991 during which they demanded state sovereignty for Ukraine.

The residents of the Donbas then found themselves as part of the newly-independent Ukrainian state. Post-independence, '…a new national ideology began to dominate in Ukraine, wherein the 'proletarian' Donbas, Russian-speaking and rooted in Soviet culture, could have only a marginal position.'[7] These problems were further exacerbated by the sharp economic downturn that accompanied the collapse of the Soviet Union, particularly felt in Donbas that had been heavily linked to 'all-Union' trade flows and investments.

Instead of the efficient, market-driven economy that the collapse of the Soviet system was supposed to bring about, what occurred in the Donbas was instead a murky form of paternalistic capitalism, in which the large industrial concerns were snapped up at bargain prices by powerful oligarchs.

Simultaneously, the Ukrainian government began replacing the Soviet symbols and pantheon of heroes with a new set of national symbols. In this period of increasing mutual misunderstanding, '...the Donbas continued to be alienated by stories of aggressive Ukrainian 'fascists' and their attempts to humiliate the region's inhabitants of by replacing their heroes with strangers, and imposing a 'wrong' version of history and 'rural' Ukrainian language and culture.'[8]

A barricade erected in Kyiv during the Euro Maidan protests in 2014. (Photograph by Dean O'Brien)

Euro Maidan

By late 2013, protests were growing on the Maidan in Kyiv against the then President of Ukraine, Donetsk-born Viktor Yanukovych. Initially, the protests were about Yanukovych's sudden U-turn on signing the European Union–Ukraine Association Agreement, instead choosing closer economic ties to the Russian Federation. However, the protests soon widened into what many protestors saw as a decision of Ukraine's path, with many on the Maidan wanting a future of closer integration with Europe and the West. The Maidan also unleashed popular anger towards the Yanukovych government and the corruption and influence of oligarchs in Ukrainian society.

A memorial to the 42 people who lost their lives during the violent clash on 2 May 2014 in Odesa, many of whom were anti-Maidan protestors. (Photograph by Dean O'Brien)

The Yanukovych government's attempt to use violence to disperse the protestors lead to violent clashes with the security forces, in which over a hundred people were killed and thousands injured. In February 2014, with his support crumbling, Yanukovych fled Ukraine for Russia, and an interim government was put in place. However, many inhabitants of eastern Ukraine, where Yanukovych had strong electoral support, viewed Yanukovych as the elected leader of Ukraine. Many therefore perceived the Maidan as the violent overthrow of a legitimate government.

A wave of anti-Maidan protests broke out across southern and eastern Ukraine, often clashing with pro-Maidan groups. In a particularly tragic event, 42 people lost their lives during such a violent clash on 2 May 2014 in Odesa. Many were anti-Maidan protestors who were killed in a fire that broke out in a building that they had taken over.

These deaths in Odesa became a rallying cry for anti-Maidan protestors in Donbas and further afield. The stage was now set for a wider confrontation in the Donbas, where anti-government sentiment was now particularly strong.

Seizure of Crimea

Following the 2014 events at the Maidan in Kyiv, Russia moved swiftly to annex the Crimean Peninsula. In the chaotic aftermath of the fall of Yanukovych, the interim Ukrainian government was disorganised and focused on internal problems. As such, the infiltration in late February 2014 of Russian special forces wearing

'Polite People' morale patch, widely available on sale in Donetsk. (Author's collection)

no insignia, came almost totally by surprise. These regular Russian Federation forces were widely referred to as 'Little Green Men' in the Western media, but more commonly referred to in the Russian media as 'Polite People'.

Many of these Russian Federation forces emerged from the Russian base of Sevastopol on the Crimean Peninsula, which had been leased to Russia by agreement after the collapse of the Soviet Union. By early March 2014, Russian forces exercised complete control over the Crimean Peninsula, cutting it off from the rest of Ukraine. They were aided by various proxy forces including what were entitled 'self-defence militias', who employed a motley array of combat equipment in stark contrast to the modern Russian equipment carried by the 'Polite People.' The mixing of regular Russian forces with local 'self-defence militias' was a technique later used on a vastly increased scale in eastern Ukraine, though with differing results.

On 16 March 2014, a referendum on Crimea's status was held across the peninsula, under the watchful eye of both the 'self-defence militias' and Russian forces. The referendum was widely condemned by the Ukrainian government and in the West. The result of this heavily-rigged referendum was overwhelmingly in favour of joining the Russian Federation, and on 17 March 2014 – in the face of wide international condemnation – Russia formally annexed Crimea into its territory.

The annexation by Russia of the Crimean Peninsula had important repercussions with direct relevance to eastern Ukraine. The rapid integration of the peninsula into the territory of the Russian Federation in the aftermath of a hurriedly organised 'referendum' undoubtedly emboldened pro-Russian elements in the Donbas, many of whom no doubt hoped a similar swift and relatively bloodless campaign might take place there. As one study of pro-Russian paramilitaries in Donbas noted, 'The expectation of 'the Crimean scenario' … that would secure the position of pro-Russian fighters was common for all groups.'[9]

However, the extent to which the lightning success of the Crimean annexation encouraged further Russian interventionism in Donbas was debated. Mark Galeotti suggested that the Kremlin's intervention in Donbas was a purposeful strategy: 'The ease of the peninsula's seizure and the disarray in Kyiv encouraged Putin and his advisors to make a fateful over-reach [in Donbas] … This was a serious miscalculation.'[10]

Others note that Russian policy in Donbas was far more limited, at least initially: 'Russia's role in the creation of the 'People's Republics' should neither be underestimated nor overestimated … Moscow did

A poster featuring a Russian Federation soldier. Those who appeared in Crimea in 2014 were often euphemistically referred to as the 'Little Green Men' or the 'Polite People'. (Photograph by Dean O'Brien)

not send large numbers of troops – like in Crimea – to achieve its goals. Instead, it deployed a limited number of agents in order to "incite, support and protect local elites and paramilitaries."[11]

Alexander Khodakovsky, who would go on to found the DPR's Vostok Regiment, '…insisted that the initial impulse was very much a local one … "Of course, afterwards, people from Russia made contact with us. Of course we were used, we became puppets. But in the beginning, it was a genuine and natural thing."'[12]

Researchers such as Anna Matveeva, who interviewed numerous members of the DPR and LPR senior leadership in 2016, similarly deduced a profound hesitancy in the Kremlin about militarily supporting the DPR and LPR uprising in Donbas, during its initial phase in 2014.

2
IDEOLOGY AND MOTIVATION

This section will explore the motivations of DPR militants who joined the armed formations. People who fought in the DPR's armed formations could be categorised into three main groups.

The first were Donbas residents, recruited locally. An important fact to note is that despite almost constant shortages of military personnel, with most of its major units constantly operating under-capacity, the DPR did not initiate general conscription to its armed formations until 19 February 2022. Therefore, during the eight year period covered by this book, it relied on 'volunteers' only.[1]

Recruitment was undertaken continuously, utilising mass media campaigns to promote the armed formations. This was reflected in the wide array of visual propaganda including posters, banners, patches and other items seen across the DPR, which gave some insight into the ideological underpinnings of the DPR. Other motivations for Donbas locals may have been economic rather than ideological, a point which will be discussed further below.

The second were international volunteers who came from abroad to join the cause – these were especially prominent in the initial phases of the conflict in 2014 and 2015. One study suggested that '…perhaps about 50,000 people went through Donbas who were non-citizens of Ukraine, and out of them 30,000 were combatants. Many of them did not stay long—there were people who came for two weeks or a month… Their combat effectiveness mostly was not great, but they manned the ranks and generated a spirit of solidarity.'[2]

International volunteers were usually more driven by the ideological foundations of the movement, and sometimes found themselves at odds with Donbas locals, who had different motivators. The international volunteers were the basis for the formation of

Recruiting poster for the DPR armed formations, Donetsk 2018. The main text reads: 'Join the ranks of the armed forces of the DPR / Serve under contract / Call the department of the military commissariat of the DPR'. The picture depicts a T-90 main battle tank, a type never reliably documented in use by the DPR. (Private collection, used with permission)

the numerous 'international brigades' which the DPR claimed among its ranks in the early days of the conflict. These included the Hungarian Legion of St Stephen and the Spanish Carlos Palomino International Brigade.[3] None of these units ever mustered more than a couple of hundred people each at most, and few lasted in any significant way past the end of 2014, by which time most of their participants had returned home.

The third were Russian Federation military personnel deployed to the DPR's armed formations to fill specialist

Red ideology. A blending of old and new symbols was common to DPR imagery. Here, an Order of the Patriotic War First Class (a Soviet Second World War-era award) is superimposed on the St George's ribbon and the Novorossiya flag. The date '9 May' refers to Victory Day. Magnet, 2016. (Author's collection)

support, command, and liaison roles. These were distinct from Russian Federation military personnel who fought in Donbas in regular Russian Federation forces deployed to the region as discrete units, in particular in the battles at Ilovaisk in 2014 and Debaltseve in early 2015.

Overall it has been estimated that among the DPR and LPR's armed formations, in the early stages of the conflict '…about 50 percent of the fighters were local to Donbas, 30 percent came from the rest of Ukraine including its western part, 10 percent were from Russia, and 10 percent from a variety of other countries. The impression of a massive presence of Russian combatants was created because many were in commanding roles, especially at first before indigenous commanders emerged.'[4]

Three Colours of Novorossiya

The historian Marlene Laruelle identified three principle strands of ideology which underpinned the two People's Republics of eastern Ukraine, which she referred to as the 'Three Colours of Novorossiya.' The three colours were red, white and brown.[5]

The red strand of ideology emphasised memory of the Soviet Union, which in the DPR was reflected in both the use of Soviet symbology, and the glorification of the industrial legacy of the Donbas. It was this strand of DPR ideology that was commonly derided by detractors as 'neo-Soviet' owing to its use of Soviet symbols, many of which related to the power and eventual victory of the Soviet Union during the Second World War.

One of the most prominent examples of 'red' ideology in the DPR was the retention of Lenin statues and other overt Soviet symbology in towns and villages under DPR control. This was contrast to the rest of Ukraine, where Lenin statues were removed under decommunization laws. Other strands of neo-Soviet, 'red' ideology in the DPR focused on Stalin and his image as a successful wartime leader. However, the use of neo-Soviet ideology by the DPR was limited and very selective – there was no 'resurrection' of Marx or Engels in the official propaganda, for example.

The white strand was based on Orthodox theocracy and the use of tsarist imagery. This form of ideology was often openly religious, and related propaganda items depicted phrases such as 'We are Russian – God is with us.' In addition, Laruelle suggested, the use of images of Tsar Nicholas II hinted a desire for a return to an earlier form of political autocracy. This strand was also closely linked to that of the 'Russian World' concept. 'Some researchers claim that it is a

Of note in the DPR was the retention of Soviet-era symbology, including statues of Lenin and reverence towards Stalin as a successful wartime leader. (Photograph by Dean O'Brien)

White ideology. 'We are Russian – God is with us.' The black, white and yellow flag in the background belonged to Imperial Russia, Tsar Nicholas II is depicted on the left. Magnet, widely available in Donetsk, 2016. (Author's collection)

Brown ideology. '300 Strelkovtsev'. Igor 'Strelkov' Girkin is the central figure depicted. Magnet, 2016. (Author's collection)

An early version of the flag of Novorossiya used by the DPR and LPR. The colours of the Imperial Russian flag are reversed, with black at the bottom. The double-headed eagle, a symbol of Russia that dates back to Byzantium, is displayed with a Soviet-style motto, 'Will and Labour.' Magnet, c. 2016. (Author's collection)

type of neo-imperialist strategy which aims to create an anti-Western and anti-democratic consolidation on the basis of the Orthodox denomination.'[6]

The brown ideological strand was based around the concept of the 'Russian Spring,' and a yearning for a form of culturally-Russian statehood reborn free of Western influence, oligarchs, and moral decadence. As Laruelle noted, this strand sublimated and glorified violence, reflected in social media posts which detailed the exploits of DPR fighters, often accompanied by combat footage and martial music. An example of propaganda linked to this type of ideology was the comparison drawn between the first DPR fighters under Igor Girkin and the popular 2006 Hollywood film '300' in which Spartan warriors held out against seemingly overwhelming odds.[7]

One notable aspect of these three 'colours' of ideology is how contradictory they could appear. As one observer of such propaganda noted: 'While many Russian nationalists and imperialists draw on imagery from both the pre- and post-Revolutionary periods, tsarist symbols continue to be anathema to diehard Communists, while Communist symbols are abhorred by most Orthodox believers.'[8]

Foundation Myths: Novorossiya, Donetsk-Krivoy Rog, and Russian Eurasianism

It is worth briefly examining the concept of Novorossiya, as it grew so central to the conflict. Literally meaning 'New Russia', the word was historically used in the Russian Empire to denote the steppe lands along the north shores of the Black Sea. These lands had been annexed by the Russian Empire under Catherine the Great in the second half of the eighteenth century.

As a modern-day political concept, as Matveeva noted, Novorossiya '...was not invented by Putin after Crimea but emerged during the dissolution of the USSR. In Odesa, a "Democratic Union of Novorossiya" was established in 1991 and campaigned for a "special state status" within its historical boundaries. The idea did not presuppose joining Russia, but was a kind of new beginning for the lands that comprised it.'[9] These ideas had little traction at the time, beyond a few supporters.

In a similar way, the concept of the Donetsk-Krivoy Rog[10] Republic was resurrected after the fall of the Soviet Union. An organisation called the International Movement for Donbas, founded at Donetsk National University in the early 1990s, and pushed for greater autonomy for Donbas.

Among its activities was historical research into the history of Donbas, as well as irredentist musings. It continued its activities despite being censured by the Ukrainian authorities, but their beliefs and objectives remained very much at the fringe of Ukrainian politics until the events of 2014. Among its founding members was Vladimir Kornilov, a historian who in 2011 published a book called *Donetsk-Krivoy Rog Republic: The Assassinated Dream*.[11] This book later became a foundation stone in the national myth-making of the DPR.

The Russian Civil War-era Donetsk-Krivoy Rog Soviet Republic was a short-lived self-proclaimed Soviet Republic that existed for a short period in 1918, laid claim to possession of far more territory than it ever controlled, and quickly vanished. For this reason, some scholars were dismissive of this foundation myth, noting that: 'In February 2018 a cycle of ceremonies took place in the DPR dedicated to the 100th anniversary of the proclamation by local Bolshevik leaders of the 'Donetsk-Krivoy Rog republic' – which never really existed.'[12]

Over a similar period, in the decade before 2014, the Russian ideologue Aleksandr Dugin was developing his theories. His work was a development on the theory of 'Eurasianism' which had been espoused by a Soviet writer called Lev Gumilev in the 1930s. Dugin developed these ideas into a neo-Eurasianism, which at its core saw Russia as a distinct cultural unit to the West.

Here too, Novorossiya was resurrected as a concept to strengthen Dugin's arguments. 'In 2009, in a nationalist prank, Dugin drew a map of a dismembered Ukraine, which included the fateful words 'Novorossiya' to signify the eastern provinces ... His use of the tsarist-era term prefigured by five years Putin's use of the same label.'[13]

These once obscure political concepts, which had spent more than a decade on the very fringes of political discourse in Russia and Ukraine, now began to come to the fore. In 2012, Putin used words from the theory of Eurasianism in a major speech. A political concept that would '...

previously, have been considered marginal and even barking mad were suddenly the anchor of ... [Putin's] most important speech of the year. And these ideas would make themselves clearer 15 months later, when Russian soldiers ... seized airports and ... chokepoints across Crimea, starting a domino effect that would lead to war in eastern Ukraine.'[14]

Donbas Identity

Another important strand to be examined when assessing the ideological motivations of DPR militants is that of the supposed 'Donbas identity.' In a pre-conflict 2007 study, it was suggested that '...one could describe most inhabitants of the Donetsk region as *tutoshnii*, that is, people whose main identification is with their locality rather than with the state or nation.'[15]

This form of self-identification was characterised as being socio-economic rather than based on ethnicity or nationality, and defied a simple dichotomy between Russian and Ukrainian identities. Similarly, '... Soviet rule [in the Donbas] produced strong identification with the locality on the one hand and the whole Soviet Union on the other, but only feeble identification with Ukraine.'[16]

This view of DPR ideological motivation places more emphasis on a localised 'Donbas identity' than ideologies connected with the wider 'Russian world' concept. As one study of DPR motivations at the beginning of the conflict noted, the establishment of the Novorossiya confederation and the People's Republics '... did not presuppose joining Russia, but was a kind of new beginning. Some rebels were saying that they were not interested in Russia's geopolitical projects, but in Donbass' future.'[17] In a similar vein, other studies of attitudes in Donbas discovered that '... mistrust toward Moscow and Kyiv were present in nearly equal measure among the region's industrial workers in 2014.'[18]

Another fact worth noting is the disappointment of some Russian ethno-nationalists who considered that '...no "Russian" (*russkii*) Spring had taken place in eastern Ukraine ... [Based] on the fact that the People's Republics of Donetsk and Lugansk had

'Our Choice – Russia!' A giant banner hanging in central Donetsk on 9 May 2019, with smaller banners celebrating five years of the DPR. The building on which the banner is hanging was, before 2014, the Hotel Liverpool, complete with Beatles-themed rooms and red phone box on the street outside. Donetsk, 9 May 2019. (Private photo collection, used with permission)

'Russian Spring'. Morale patch, widely available in Donetsk, c. 2016. (Author's collection)

been proclaimed in the name of their "multiethnic population," not in the name of the "*russkii*" people.'[19]

Again, contrary to the focus placed by Western observers on the Russian Federation's defence of 'ethnic Russians' in their near abroad, in this case DPR ideological motivation favoured a more inclusive multi-ethnic approach suited to the DPR's population, rather than a narrower ethnic Russian basis.

Overall, it is difficult to unpick to what extent the utilisation of the 'Donbas identity' and foundation myths relating to the region were brought to the fore later, as a response to the failure of the hoped-for 'Crimea scenario' which would have seen the region swiftly and directly annexed by the Russian Federation.

Similarly, it was noted that the very existence of the two People's Republics in eastern Ukraine, and the failure of the Novorossiya 'confederation' project, also cast doubt on the political and ideological commitment to the so-called 'Donbas identity' as the two People's Republics were unable to form a single, coherent political entity – i.e. Novorossiya – even in the face of an immediate existential threat from the Ukrainian state and its armed forces.

Economic Motivations

It is worth considering that the motivation for many of the members of the DPR's armed formations was likely to have been economic rather than ideological. As discussed above, the success of the Donbas's heavy industries was dependent on the region's important strategic position within the Soviet Union, and a decline in these heavy industries was already under way when the Soviet Union collapsed.

This economic decline continued under independent Ukraine, and after the beginning of the conflict in 2014, many of the remaining industries in the DPR were shuttered, or worked only at minimal capacity. Reports were common of salaries being many months in arrears, or staff being refused any form of leave by their employers.

In comparison to this, the stable and reliable salaries offered for service in the DPR's armed formations, reportedly the Russian rouble equivalent of approximately $230 to $390 per month in 2019,[20] would have seemed attractive to many. Research of online advertisements for DPR armed formation positions indicated salaries of 15,000 to 19,000 Russian roubles for privates and 19,500 to 25,000 roubles for sergeants, as well as social benefits such as the promise of paid vacations, free accommodation, food and healthcare, and uniform provided.[21] Such salaries compared favourably to the prevailing minimum wage in the DPR at the time, around 2,500 roubles or $40.

The academic Taras Kuzio suggested that: 'The separatists attracted those who had been marginalised by the post-Soviet

A large mural depicts a DPR militant holding a child. Central Donetsk, October 2017. (Private photo collection, used with permission)

transition who were often people with lower education, unemployed and poor who had nostalgia for the USSR.'[22]

Thus, in common with many analogous conflicts, membership of the DPR's armed formations may have been the only attractive option for many individuals, given the lack of any employment elsewhere. This lack of alternatives was possibly in many cases a stronger motivating factor than ideology.

Conclusion

The wide number of possible ideological drivers for involvement in the armed formations of the DPR was something recognised, and even encouraged, by the DPR itself. By creating a 'broad church' in terms of its ideological foundations, the DPR could attract fighters from across a broad spectrum, both from within Donbas and abroad.

Writing in the early stages of the conflict about the motivation of the armed groups that would later coalesce into the armed formations of the DPR, Igor Girkin noted: 'The irregular army gathers individuals of different opinions, united by a common Russian language and hatred against Ukraine. It is injurious for our common deal to create any common ideology for them.'[23]

As the DPR began to coalesce in Sloviansk and Donetsk in 2014, its narrative '…absorbed different ideological ingredients from monarchism to Sovietism, reflecting the kaleidoscope of identities which came together in a single social movement… . Lack of coherence made no difference in 2014 when the rebels implicitly understood what united them.'[24]

However, this lack of a coherent ideology later contributed to the disorganisation and infighting manifested within the DPR after 2014, as various factions with vastly differing ideology and objectives vied for power.

3
PROPAGANDA AND SYMBOLOGY

As noted above, memory of the Second World War, and the glory and military might of the Soviet Union during that conflict, feature highly in DPR ideology and propaganda. In short, DPR propaganda often seeks to draw direct parallels between that conflict – and in particular the eventual Soviet victory in 1945 – and the ongoing struggle against the Ukrainian government.

In doing this, the DPR adopted a form of the 'extreme politicisation' of the symbols of the Second World War that has taken place in the Russian Federation, encouraged by Putin. Celebration of victory in the Second World War highlighted Russia's place as '…inheritor of the Soviet Union's great-power status. A through line follows from the Soviet victory in the Second World War to the exploration of space and the Cold War rivalry with the United States: in this worldview, what matters is the history of the empire and the power of the state.'[1]

As in Russia, a particularly important celebration in the DPR calendar is the 9 May victory parade, held annually in central Donetsk and attended by tens of thousands of spectators. As the Russian academic Medvedev notes: 'An even more surprising transformation of the holiday is that the Russian aggression in Ukraine is justified in the name of the Victory … Propaganda has created in people's minds a virtual continuation of the Great Patriotic War in the shape of the war in the Donbass; where the Ukrainians have been given the role of the fascists.'[2]

After a column of military equipment, usually led by Second World War-era vehicles including a T-34 tank, the 9 May parade in Donetsk usually included a march of the 'Immortal Regiment'.

In Donetsk it became common for relatives of those who had fallen since 2014 to participate in the Victory Day Parade. This photo shows a woman carrying photos of a dead relative on Victory Day in May 2019. Note the use of the St. George's Ribbon alongside the pictures. (Photograph by Dean O'Brien)

Senior members of the DPR leadership watching the march of the 'Immortal Regiment' passing the review stand on Lenin Square in Donetsk, 9 May 2018. In the front row, from left to right, is: Sergey Velikorodny, Deputy Defence Minister; Vladimir Kononov, Defence Minister; and Aleksander Zakharchenko, Head of the DPR. (Private photo collection, used with permission)

The 'Immortal Regiment' event started in Russia in 2012, as a participatory event in which people march on Victory Day bearing pictures of relatives who participated in the Second World War.[3]

In Donetsk, and in other major cities in the DPR, such parades included people bearing pictures of relatives who died during the fighting since the 2014 conflict began, again almost seamlessly blending collective memory of the 'Great Patriotic War' with the ongoing struggle against the Ukrainian government.

Flags

Two flags predominated on the uniforms and vehicles of the DPR's armed formations. The first flag was that of Novorossiya, which

'Novorossiya' flag patch, full colour, c. 2016. (Author's collection)

Early version 'DPR' flag patch, full colour, c. 2016. Later versions of the flag dispensed with the writing, and then with the double-headed eagle crest, in favour of a much simpler tricolour design. (Author's collection)

Late version 'DPR' flag patch, subdued variant, c. 2018. (Author's collection)

continued to be used despite the overall failure of the Novorossiya confederation project. The second was that of the DPR itself. Like the modern political concepts of Novorossiya and the DPR, both flags actually predated the start of the conflict by several years.

The Novorossiya flag, commonly seen on uniforms across both the DPR and LPR, was designed in 2013 by pro-Russian activists. Dugin, the Russian Eurasianist ideologue, apparently '…correctly predicted the design of the flag … red with a blue St Andrew's cross – two months before a contest was held to decide it[4]'.

The DPR flag is not – as commonly thought – that of the 1918 Donetsk-Krivoy Rog Republic, whose history has been briefly discussed above. Its provenance is, like that of the Novorossiya flag, much more modern, and '…the flag used by the Donetsk People's Republic is, with alterations, that of the International Movement for Donbas or the *Interdvizheniye Donbasa*, an organisation whose roots started only in August 1989, in a lecture theatre of Donetsk University.'[5]

Subdued versions of the Novorossiya and DPR flags were common on the combat uniforms of DPR armed formation militants. Full-coloured patches were mainly used for parades or by non-frontline units.

St. George's Ribbon

The most common piece of DPR symbology, shared with the LPR, was the widespread use of the St. George's ribbon. In many ways closely linked to the Immortal Regiment, the St. George's ribbon was a relatively 'new' piece of symbology, which originated in Russia in 2005.

This black and orange ribbon became a key piece of DPR symbology. 'The ribbon is modelled on a high-ranking order instituted by the Stalin regime in 1942. It has the same colours as the Soviet medal but a different name: the Soviet prototype was called 'Order of the Guard' (*gvardeiskii orden*) … Both the Order itself as

Here the St. George's ribbon is seen again, this time on the grave of a DPR soldier. (Photograph by Dean O'Brien)

Here the St. George's Ribbon is used as a marking on the side of a BMP-2 infantry fighting vehicle during the May 2019 Victory Day Parade. (Photograph by Dean O'Brien)

A St George's ribbon entwined with the DPR colours. Donbas, 2017. (Private photo collection, used with permission)

well as various kinds of ornamentation in orange and black featured on numerous wartime and post-war posters and postcards'.[6]

The orange and black St George's ribbon became so synonymous with the People's Republics of the DPR and LPR that the production of such ribbons was banned in Ukraine.[7] At the start of the conflict in 2014 in Sloviansk, the ribbon seemed to emerge as a distinguishing symbol for the proto-DPR armed formations, as noted by Artem Shevchenko: 'There were separatists' paraphernalia in almost every town, such as notorious brown-and-black St. George's ribbons, Russian tricolors, black-blue-and-red flags of the still to be proclaimed "Donetsk People's Republic", and other symbols of different illegal groups operating in the region.'[8]

In the DPR, the St George's ribbon was the unifying symbol used on posters and on the sides of vehicles and weapons in the Victory Day parades. In this sense, the St. George's ribbon could be considered a wildly successful piece of 'political technology' – one of a couple of symbols universally adopted across both of the People's Republics in eastern Ukraine.

As Kolstø noted '… the ambiguous quality of the ribbon symbol makes it possible to sell it to different ideological groups in Russian society ranging from conservatives, monarchists and Orthodox to Communists and Soviet nostalgics. Presenting it as harkening back to tsarist times *and* to the Second World War at the same time was clearly intentional and highly successful.'[9]

4
STRATEGIC AIMS OF THE DPR AND THE RUSSIAN FEDERATION

The actual strategic goals of the DPR as an entity were not as immediately apparent as one might expect. Though often described as separatist, in fact a wide range of strategic goals were stated over the years by the DPR and its principal actors, including: full autonomy as an independent state, desire for full annexation by Russia, and reincorporation into Ukraine as an autonomous entity under a federal system.

This last option may seem surprising given the common appellation of the DPR as 'separatist,' but the effective federalisation of Ukraine was in fact one of the aims of the Minsk II agreement, and was thought of as being more in line with probable Russian foreign policy objectives at the beginning of the conflict in 2014. In this way, an autonomous and pro-Kremlin Donbas, within a federalised Ukraine, would have been able to veto Ukrainian moves towards closer integration with the EU and NATO.

Alexander Khodakovsky, who founded and commanded the DPR's Vostok Regiment, was reported to have favoured the idea of eventual reconciliation with Ukraine, via emplacing a 'concrete wall' in between the two sides for 20 years to allow mutual hatreds to cool, and then negotiating.[1]

Other senior members of the DPR also stressed that '…common identity in their view does not imply negation of "Ukrainian-ness" and that a cultural conquest or a territorial homeland was not what they were fighting for'[2] and in this view, the regimes in Kyiv and Moscow were equally complicit in the suffering in Donbas.

As the 11 May 2014 DPR referendum started, the Polish journalist Pieniążek, who was on the ground at the time, noted that for many voters the referendum was '…simply an opportunity to express their disagreement with Kiev's politics, but this doesn't necessarily mean they want their regions to separate from Ukraine. They often talk about federalization, but in fact they would be happy with simply decentralization. They claim they want a stronger say in electing the authorities and that the referendum is a means to achieve this.'[3]

Perhaps one of the most far-reaching goals ever publicly stated by the DPR was outlined in an announcement by Zakharchenko in 2017, which included the aim to create a new state called 'Malorossiya.'[4] This bizarre concept, entirely divorced from the military and political realities facing the DPR at the time, envisioned a new state encompassing most of the territory of Ukraine, but with its new capital in Donetsk instead of Kyiv.

A map of this imaginary political entity was presented, as well as a new flag. Some Western observers thought that this declaration might have been at the whim of Moscow, in order to help present the conflict as a civil war.[5] However as others noted, '…the idea, which was seemingly not coordinated with Luhansk or Moscow, was quietly dropped weeks later.'[6]

More immediately, the DPR aimed for 'administrative' control of the territory within the boundaries of Ukraine's Donetsk oblast, and – with echoes of other territorial conflicts elsewhere in the world – referred to those parts of Donetsk oblast under Ukrainian government control as areas 'temporarily occupied by the Ukrainian armed forces.'

Russian strategic goals in Donbas

As Igor Girkin himself found in 2014, though the Kremlin gave its tacit blessing to his mission, the hoped-for Crimea scenario involving large scale deployment of Russian Federation forces and subsequent complete annexation did not occur.

Despite later committing significant resources and ground forces in order to prevent the military defeat of the DPR and LPR in 2014 and early 2015, the Kremlin refused to recognise either entity, or to immediately and completely annex them as it had done with Crimea. In time, it also quietly dropped public support for the 'Novorossiya' confederation project as well.

The Kremlin expressed support for the Minsk Agreements signed in 2014 and 2015, but also insisted that the Ukrainian government deal with the DPR and LPR directly. As the fighting ebbed and flowed along the contact line in the years between 2015 and 2022, Putin maintained that the causes of the conflict were '…rooted in long-simmering discontent in the Donbass and social and political cleavages within modern Ukraine.

'Time to go back, Donbass.' Magnet, c. 2016. Such imagery, depicting the Russian flag and the total pre-2014 area of both Donetsk and Luhansk oblasts, reflected the desire of some in the DPR to be annexed by the Russian Federation. (Author's collection)

Aspirational cartography. A map depicting the territory of Ukraine, with the entire territories of the oblasts of Luhansk and Donetsk painted in the colours of their respective 'People's Republics'. Crimea has been marked with the words 'Russian Federation' and the colours of the Russian flag. Luhansk, 2017. (Private photo collection, used with permission)

This version of events … made Russia a concerned observer but ultimately an external actor.'[7]

This resulted in an ongoing discussion, primarily in Western circles, about exactly what Russian strategic goals in Donbas were. As Bettina Renz and Hanna Smith noted, the '…idea of a 'guessing game' clearly indicates there are various conflicting explanations for Russian conduct: Russia is after the Azov Sea coastline; Russia is building up historical Novorossiya; Russia is creating on purpose a new frozen conflict; … Russia wants Ukraine to back away from EU integration; or Russia is just simply cooking up a strategy as it goes along.'[8]

It is also important not to project Russian strategic goals backwards, in light of the February 2022 'special military operation' in Ukraine, and to assume that the stated or eventual goals of that massive assault were the Kremlin's strategic plan all along. Since 2008, the Kremlin's aggressive military interventions abroad in Ukraine and Syria have been '…largely improvised, focused on short-term tactical thinking rather than any longer-term project. The apparent aggression stems not from a growing confidence, but from a pervasive and deepening anxiety about Russian weakness.'[9]

Regarding Russia's overall strategy in Donbas from 2014 to 2022, this book accepts the theory put forwards by Sutyagin and Bronk in 2017 as the most likely: 'Moscow's ultimate political goal there is to insert the 'rebel republics' back into the fabric of the Ukrainian state while maintaining full control over them. This would force Kiev to accept the rebel territories' de facto right of veto over Ukrainian policy.'[10]

5
KEY BATTLES AND THE FORMATION OF UNITS

In this section, some of the key battles of the conflict in eastern Ukraine between April 2014 and February 2022 will be examined. This is by no means an exhaustive account of all the battles that took place in these years of conflict, but will provide a summary of those battles in which many early units of what would later become the armed formations of the DPR took part.

Early Events in Donetsk (March – April 2014)

As protests against the Ukrainian government spread in Donetsk, several hitherto inconspicuous individuals experienced a meteoric rise to power. In front of crowds of protestors in Donetsk on 1 March 2014, Pavel Gubarev, a graduate of Donetsk National University who had managed a company supplying costumed Ded Moroz (Santa Claus) actors, proclaimed himself People's Governor and leader of

'Donbass People's Militia'. An early name and logo for the 2014 armed units that later came together into the DPR's armed formations, and eventually DPR 1st Army Corps. Magnet, c. 2015. (Author's collection)

the 'Donbass People's Militia' – a catchall phrase for the forerunner to the armed formations of the DPR that coalesced later on.

Gubarev then lead protestors who captured the Donetsk Regional Administration Building in the centre of Donetsk. However, at the time the Ukrainian SBU was still able to operate in Donetsk, and Gubarev was arrested on 6 March 2014. He would not be released until May 2014, in a prisoner exchange with some SBU officers who had been captured by the DPR.

Alexander Zakharchenko had worked in the coal mining industry, and had become head of the Oplot sporting club in Donetsk, which would later become the Oplot Brigade. In the confused, chaotic and violent events of March and April, he led his Oplot supporters in storming the Donetsk city council building.

Another early DPR leader was '…Aleksandr Borodai, a writer and editor of *Zavtra* who would later turn up as a Russian leader of the separatist revolt in eastern Ukraine in April 2014. Both he and his friend, Igor Girkin, had fought in Moldova for Transnistria's pro-Moscow rebels.'[1]

Elsewhere, as Richard Sakwa wrote: 'The leadership of the insurgency was a motley crew. They included Denys Pushilin, one of the organisers of the MMM pyramid scheme in Donetsk in the 1990s, while Nikolai Solntsev, a technologist at a meat-processing plant, became the DPR's ideology minister.'[2]

The Polish journalist Paweł Pieniążek, who was in Donbas during 2014, noted how the protests spread across the region, causing a rising wave of participation. In the economically depressed Donbas,

Aleksander Zakharchenko, Head of the DPR. Postcard no. 2 in the set 'Gold Star Heroes', issued by the DPR Ministry of Communication, 2017. (Author's collection)

he noted, it was easier for the DPR leaders '…to find support among populations struggling with serious social problems. It is also easier to project an impression of mass involvement and total control. Pro-Russian demonstrations in Donetsk coincide with demonstrations in Alchevsk, Khartsyzk, Druzhkivka, Horlivka, Kramatorsk, Makiivka, and Slovyansk. They also erupt in two larger cities, Luhansk and Mariupol.'[3]

Sloviansk (12 April 2014 – 5 July 2014)

The actions of Igor 'Strelkov' Girkin at Sloviansk formed the spark which lit the conflict in the Donbas. The extent to which Girkin's actions were approved by Moscow is uncertain, but the researcher Anna Matveeva, who interviewed Girkin in person in 2016, thought it likely that '…the intentions of Strelkov and his comrades-in-arms were probably known in Moscow but the mission was not ordered… That allowed for the Kremlin to distance itself from the armed group in case their adventure would not generate local traction.'[4]

Girkin became a charismatic symbol for the early forces of what became the DPR, and his character looms large over early accounts of the conflict. He dressed in White Russian uniforms, having participated in military re-enactment groups earlier in his life, and was a keen student of Russian Civil War history.

Slavyansk Garrison insignia. Full colour patch, c. 2016. There is some uncertainty as to whether this was an early unit of the Donbass People's Militia, likely absorbed into the 1st Slavic Brigade, or an 'honorary' patch worn later by those militants who took part in the battle for Sloviansk in 2014. (Author's collection)

His reported active links to the FSB and GRU were widely overstated, and allowed him to utilise a great degree of bluff in the initial phases of the operation to take control of Sloviansk. Locals who flocked to his cause thought that the Kremlin was fully behind Girkin's operation and would soon come to their aid, and in a similar way the Ukrainian authorities feared that a full-scale Russian invasion was imminent and acted more timidly than they otherwise might.

The battle for Sloviansk started on 12 April 2014, when masked militants under the command of Girkin took control of various important government buildings in the strategically important city of Sloviansk. This was Girkin's so-called 'Crimea Company', '...whose members were either renegades from the Crimean units of the UAF or Crimean volunteers.'[5] This initial group of militants probably numbered only around 50 men, however they were soon augmented by locals who joined the cause.

Sloviansk was probably chosen by Girkin as the place for the initial insertion of the 'Crimea Company' owing to several reasons. In particular, as a communication hub, at the junction of several major highways, it would be the perfect place to consolidate control of Donetsk oblast, and threaten other major Ukrainian cities such as Kharkiv and Dnipro.

In addition, the Sloviansk's very name lent itself to propagandistic purposes, a reference to Slavic unity and the 'shared civilisational space' of Russia and Ukraine, and its proximity to an important Orthodox holy site at Sviyatogirsk. Girkin and his supporters hoped that other rebellions would take place elsewhere in Ukraine, but the

People's Republics declared in Kharkiv and was quickly crushed by the Ukrainian security forces.

It also seems that Sloviansk was chosen for its manageable size, with Girkin recognising that, at least initially, he would have very limited support. In the 2016 interview he noted that his small group '...would have been lost in a large city like Donetsk. Unlike in my other wars, I barely knew the local terrain and had no information sources of my own... We thought about going to Shakhtyorsk at first, but were told that there were no local supporters there. So we decided to go to Slavyansk. There was no time to prepare.'[6]

In marked comparison to the takeover of Crimea, Western journalists noted the differing appearance of the forces who had seized control of Sloviansk in the name of the Donetsk People's Republic. A journalist from *Time* magazine noted that they '... appear to be made up mostly of war veterans, itinerant pro-Russian nationalists and ethnic Cossacks from across the former Soviet Union.'[7] Russian media sources insisted that any Russian nationals involved were there purely as 'volunteers' and on this occasion it was truer than it had been in Crimea. In this way Russia sought to maintain a greater degree of plausible deniability, at least in these initial phases of the conflict.

With Ukrainian forces pushed out of the city, a People's Mayor of Sloviansk was appointed, Vyacheslav Ponomarev, a native of Sloviansk who had been a manager of a soap factory. 'Black hoodie with the ribbon of Saint George attached, black polo shirt, black cap, and jeans – this is Ponomarev's typical outfit.'[8]

DPR rule in Sloviansk was punctuated by violence and brutality, including the murder of Ukrainian politician Volodymyr Rybak in April 2014, and the torture and subsequent murder of four members of the Pentecostal Church in June 2014.[9] The latter crime was allegedly perpetrated by the Russian Orthodox Army, an early DPR armed formation which was later absorbed into Oplot Brigade.

On 10 June 2014, Ponomarev was detained by Girkin, and largely vanished from the DPR political scene. He would be one of the first in a long line of senior DPR leaders to be 'removed' from power, by means ranging from forcible exile to targeted assassination.

The seizure of various government buildings in and around Sloviansk gave the militants and their local supporters access to large numbers of small arms. However, in the vicinity of Sloviansk, in Bakhmut, Ukrainian forces retained control of a large military depot of armoured vehicles, as well as a huge underground depot in the village of Parakeyivka reportedly containing several million small arms.[10] As more and more weapons began to arrive in the hands of the militants, this made their claims to have captured them all even more implausible.

Start of the ATO and the Ukrainian Recapture of Sloviansk (April 2014)

On 16 April 2014, the Ukrainian government launched what it called an Anti-Terrorist Operation (ATO) in Donbas, in an attempt to wrest control back from the DPR and LPR. The initial Ukrainian response was confused and hampered by chain of command problems, and as a result the militants had time to consolidate their positions.

The militants were also able to capture a number of Ukrainian armoured fighting vehicles, including BMD-1 and BMD-2 infantry fighting vehicles. However, even with the 200 or so Donbas locals who had joined the ranks of Girkin's Crimea Company, '...the gunmen did not have enough forces for the full control of the key locations ... in the densely populated agglomeration of Slovyansk-Kramatorsk.'[11]

Girkin had evidently badly overestimated the amount of support that would be forthcoming from the local population. Later in May 2014, he '…complained in a video address that he could not raise "even a thousand" local volunteers in Donetsk province to fight at the front.'[12] Furthermore, the hoped-for uprisings in Ukrainian cities further west had either been crushed or not materialised.[13]

By 24 April 2014, Ukrainian forces had almost surrounded the city, and on 2 May 2014, the Ukrainians launched an offensive to recapture Sloviansk. At this time, the number of armed DPR militants was estimated by the Ukrainians to be around 800. As the situation grew increasingly desperate, Girkin appealed to the DPR leaders Borodai and Zakharchenko, who had by then consolidated their positions in Donetsk, to launch a military operation to relieve Sloviansk.[14] This was not forthcoming, and the threat of total encirclement by Ukrainian forces loomed.

DPR Referendum

On 11 May 2014, in those areas by then under DPR control, a referendum was held. The original planned wording of the referendum would have been annexation by the Russian Federation, but the Kremlin had refused to support this, and the wording was changed to a usefully ambiguous Russian word stressing 'self-rule' or 'independence' depending on its interpretation.

Popular support was overwhelmingly for the notion, in part of course owing to the DPR's control over the process, in part because pro-Ukrainian citizens in the areas where the referendum was held boycotted the process altogether, and in part reflecting the political opinion of a significant proportion of the population.

On 5 July 2014, Sloviansk was recaptured by the Ukrainians from the DPR. Igor Girkin and the surviving DPR militants managed to escape from Sloviansk towards Donetsk. The sudden withdrawal of Girkin and the remnants of his forces evidently caught the Ukrainian ATO forces off guard, as they were not able to block or impede his withdrawal.

Around the same time, the Ukrainian armed forces also recaptured other major cities in the vicinity of Sloviansk, including Kramatorsk and Bakhmut. In Donetsk, key sites in the city had swiftly fallen under DPR control, and Borodai and Zakharchenko had been quickly able to consolidate their power there. As such, Girkin received a frosty welcome in Donetsk, where other DPR leaders and commanders had been developing their own distinct power bases and identities.

First Battle of Donetsk Airport (May 2014)

Though most of Donetsk city was under DPR control, a notable outlier was Donetsk International Airport, which remained under Ukrainian control. In late May 2014, elements of the Vostok Battalion attempted to seize the airport in what became known as the First Battle of Donetsk Airport.

Situated on the northern edges of Donetsk city, the Donetsk Sergey Prokofiev International Airport, which had been extensively rebuilt and modernised as part of the Euro 2012 football championship, now became the scene of intense fighting. On 26 May 2014, fighters from the Vostok Battalion seized the terminal buildings, only to be repulsed by the Ukrainian armed forces the following day. The Ukrainians were supported by considerable airpower, including close air support from Su-25 and MiG-29 aircraft, and Mil-24 attack helicopters.

The Vostok Battalion, and supporting Russian Spetsnaz troops from the FSB's 'Iskra' sabotage unit, were beaten back from the airport, after approximately 50 DPR and Russian fighters were killed.[15] Many of the DPR/Russian casualties were reported to have been killed in a 'friendly fire' incident by the Vostok Battalion itself. The Ukrainian armed forces retained control of the airport until September of the same year.

With the exception of the airport, the city of Donetsk was soon firmly in control of the DPR, but the Ukrainian armed forces sought to slowly encircle the city, thereby cutting it off from resupply. This also reflected a deliberate Ukrainian strategy to cleave the Donbas in two, separating the DPR and LPR from each other. During this period of the fighting in the early stages of the ATO, the Ukrainian armed forces had the advantage in terms of numbers and materiel, as well as the use of air assets.

Donetsk Airport. Magnet, widely available in Donetsk c. 2016. Such 'before and after' photomontage showing the destruction wrought by the war was common in the DPR. (Author's collection)

However, the use of heavy firepower by the Ukrainian armed forces, including artillery, MLRS and airstrikes, caused casualties and suffering among the civilian population in Donbas, and in many cases spurred recruitment to the DPR and LPR's armed formations. This was reinforced by the tactics used by the DPR's armed formations during this period, who used speed and agility to fire from residential areas and then escape before Ukrainian return fire landed, often causing civilian casualties.

On 2 June 2014, a Ukrainian airstrike on central Luhansk using Su-25 ground attack aircraft killed eight people. The attack was a psychological shock to many of the inhabitants of Donbas, and acted as a catalyst for support for the armed formations.

However, what the DPR and LPR referred to as *voentorg*,[16] the supply of weaponry, ammunition and supplies by the Russian Federation to the DPR's armed formations, was at this time still relatively constricted. This mirrored the ambivalence of the Kremlin towards the Novorossiya project as a whole, and as Matveeva noted, '…Moscow hesitated for a long time about supplying weapons to the rebels beyond those seized in Crimea. It did not know whom it could trust, because it was hard to be sure which of the no-name warlords apart from Strelkov and Borodai were reliable, could handle complex weaponry and were not outright bandits.'[17]

Battle at Savur-Mohyla (June – August 2014)

As the Ukrainian armed forces and the DPR's armed formations battled for control of the hinterland between Donetsk and the border with the Russian Federation, a battle occurred over the hill at Savur-Mohyla.

At just over 270m high, the hill was important as a strategic outpost commanding the surrounding terrain. It was equally important as a symbolic prize for the DPR, as Soviet troops had battled over it in August 1943. On the hill stood a memorial complex built in 1963, commemorating the Soviet soldiers who had fallen there. Crowning the summit of the hill was a huge obelisk alongside which was a stylised statue of a Soviet soldier.

DPR militants took up position on and around the hill on 7 June 2014, to help protect the nearby highway which was an important supply route to the border with the Russian Federation. Ukrainian forces who were attempting to encircle Donetsk fought DPR forces for the hill, with control changing hands several times over the course of the battle.

During the fighting in late August the obelisk collapsed under heavy shelling, and on 26 August 2014 the DPR claimed it was finally in control of the hill. On the summit of the hill after the battle was a small graveyard containing the graves of those DPR militants who were killed in the battle.

Change in DPR Leadership (August 2014)

By August 2014, towns and cities on the outskirts of Donetsk were being recaptured by the Ukrainian armed forces, and Donetsk city itself was under Ukrainian artillery fire. To the Ukrainians, it seemed that military victory was only a matter of days away.

Igor Girkin appealed to Russia for more support in order to prevent the total defeat of the DPR. On the 14 August 2014, he resigned as Minister of Defence of the DPR.[18] His resignation closely followed the replacement of Alexander Borodai by Alexander Zakharchenko as Prime Minister of the DPR on 7 August 2014.

'Eventually the Russian leaders of the Donetsk Republic were prudently replaced by Ukrainians. First Strelkov resigned … Then Boroday was replaced by the Ukrainian Alexander Zakharchenko … Zakharchenko insisted on coming to cabinet meetings dressed

The memorial complex at Savur-Mohyla showing recent battle damage. (Photographs by Dean O'Brien)

in camouflage and sporting the Cross of St George (4th Class), a Russian military decoration.'[19]

These resignations of key DPR leaders represented a new phase in the conflict. As well as the evident military weakness of the irregular DPR armed formations in the face of the larger and better-equipped Ukrainian armed forces, there was a political reason for replacing Girkin and Borodai, both of whom were Russian citizens. 'By August [2014], it was clear the separatists were on the precipice of failure, and a negotiated settlement with Ukraine would prove difficult to orchestrate given that the leaders of the separatist republics were both Russian citizens (i.e., externally introduced actors who could

Eternal Memory of Heroes. The photo depicts the pre-2014 memorial complex at Savur-Mohyla. Magnet, c. 2018. (Author's collection)

A small cemetery atop Savur-Mohyla containing the graves of those DPR militants killed in the battle. (Photograph by Dean O'Brien)

The remnants of the destroyed obelisk on the summit of Savur-Mohyla. The graffiti on the base reads: 'It's Our DPR – Land – Strength.' July 2017. (Private photo collection, used with permission)

not negotiate on behalf of the breakaway regions). In effect, the facade of a locally inspired rebellion became pointless.'[20]

Direct Russian Intervention at Ilovaisk (August 2014)

By early August 2014, the Ukrainian armed forces, including a number of volunteer battalions, were advancing from the south towards the small town of Ilovaisk. This small town, around 30 kilometres southeast of Donetsk, had a pre-war population of some 18,000 and was notable as being a major railway town on one of the main lines between Donetsk and the Russian Federation.

Ilovaisk had been captured by DPR forces during the opening stages of the conflict in April 2014, but now in the face of the advancing Ukrainian forces, the DPR's armed formations – including Somalia Battalion, as well as elements of Slavyansk and Oplot – were forced to cede part of the town to the Ukrainian forces on the 18 and 19 August. Intense street fighting broke out.[21]

The successful recapture of Ilovaisk by the Ukrainian armed forces raised the spectre of the possible encirclement of Donetsk, and the likely subsequent total defeat of the DPR. With Ilovaisk retaken, Ukrainian forces were now just 50 kilometres south of the town of Debaltseve – also a major rail hub – which was then still under Ukrainian control. However, further Ukrainian thrusts in that direction were blocked by the DPR's armed formations.

The overall weakness of the DPR's nascent and irregular armed formations in the face of Ukrainian mechanised armed forces, as well as the inability to recruit as many soldiers to the ranks of the DPR as initially anticipated, meant that the Kremlin then chose to commit significant ground forces to eastern Ukraine in order to prevent the DPR's total collapse. As one analyst noted, at this point 'Russia threw caution to the side and sent well-supplied armored columns into the fray to stabilize the situation and to preserve its proxy.'[22]

On the 24 August 2014, Russian mechanised ground forces crossed the border into Ukraine and entered Donetsk oblast at various points, with some advancing towards Ilovaisk. As a result, the Ukrainian armed forces in the town themselves became encircled, and heavy fighting ensued. A siege of the town resulted in heavy casualties among both the Ukrainian units and the civilian population now trapped in the city. Attempts to break the siege were thwarted by DPR/Russian artillery bombardments and ground forces.

'Mariupol is Ukraine': pro-Ukrainian mural in Mariupol. (Photograph by Dean O'Brien)

Almost simultaneously, a column of Russian ground forces entered the southern part of Donetsk oblast, and advanced along the coastline. They seized the coastal town of Novoazovsk on 27 August 2014 and, continuing west, threatened the vital port city of Mariupol. With its deep port and massive steel plants accounting for a large proportion of the economic output of the Donbas, Mariupol represented an important target for the DPR and Russian forces. Its capture would have allowed the creation of a more self-sustaining and economically viable political entity.

Mariupol itself was successfully defended by the Ukrainian armed forces, but Ukraine was compelled to abandon a long stretch of the border of Donetsk oblast with the Russian Federation, ceding a long swath of territory to the DPR from Starobesheve in the north to Novoazovsk in the south. By opening a new front in the conflict, the Russians also relieved pressure on DPR forces at Ilovaisk.

Under a brokered peace deal, it was agreed that Ukrainian units would leave encircled Ilovaisk and move along pre-agreed safe routes to Ukrainian-controlled territory. However, as the remaining Ukrainian forces withdrew, they were fired upon by the combined DPR and Russian forces, resulting in what was officially reported as around 350 casualties. The true number of casualties may never be known, but is thought by some to be 10 times higher.

The siege of Ilovaisk proved a turning point in the conflict, as Russia moved to a more conventional form of conflict by deploying significant ground forces in order to prevent the military defeat of the DPR. The battle at Ilovaisk was the defining moment which secured the future of the DPR as a political entity, and utterly altered the balance of power between the Ukrainian state and the DPR.

The catastrophic Ukrainian losses at 'Ilovaisk Cauldron' (as it became known) had a profound political impact in Ukraine. In addition to the grim toll of military casualties, the territorial gains of the Ukrainian ATO were rolled back in the face of reinvigorated DPR armed formations who had been massively reinforced by Russian ground forces and supported by cross-border artillery fire. New swaths of territory had been ceded to the DPR in the southern parts of Donetsk oblast, and the Ukrainian armed forces had lost their strategic momentum and were now on a defensive footing.

DPR Capture of Donetsk Airport (January 2015)

The DPR began a second concerted effort to gain control of Donetsk Airport in late September 2014. The Somalia and Sparta Battalions were heavily involved in the subsequent battles, as well as Vostok. As the use of artillery was crucial for both sides in the battle, and specific Russian military support was evident in the form of 1RL232 and 1RL239 radar systems, identified near the airport at the time, which enabled the DPR to better target its counter-battery fire.

Heavy fighting ensued in and around the old and new terminal buildings. The airport was almost completely destroyed in the fighting, and at some point the tall control tower collapsed under the weight of bombardment. Towards the end of the siege, the fighting was occurring floor by floor.

The stubborn defence of the Ukrainian armed forces soldiers who held on to the terminal buildings earned them the grudging admiration of DPR and Russian forces, who gave them the nickname 'Cyborgs'. When the airport was finally taken by the DPR in its entirety, on 21st January 2015, it was a major propaganda victory for the DPR.

It also represented an important tactical prize, as the Ukrainian armed forces were forced to pull back to defensive lines in Pisky on the northern side of the runway. Additionally, Ukrainian artillery was now pushed back much further from the populated

He defeated the Cyborgs. Magnet, c. 2016. The Soviet-era cartoon figure of Cheburashka, famous for his oversized ears, was widely used by the DPR. Here Cheburashka is wearing the flag of Novorossiya, while the caption makes a reference to the defeat of the Ukrainian armed forces at Donetsk Airport. (Author's collection)

areas of Donetsk city. This meant that the DPR now controlled the urban conurbation of Donetsk pretty much in its entirety, with the Ukrainian armed forces occupying positions in the surrounding fields and small villages.

Capture of Debaltseve (January – February 2015)

Debaltseve is a small town in Donetsk oblast, situated very close to the border with neighbouring Luhansk oblast. With a pre-war population of some 24,000 people, its importance was very much as a road and railway junction town, on the lines of communication between Donetsk and Luhansk oblasts. Initially seized by proto-DPR armed formations in the early stages of the conflict in April 2014, it had been recaptured by the Ukrainian armed forces in July 2014 during the initial stages of the Anti-Terrorist Operation.

By January 2015, Ukrainian armed forces in Debaltseve were surrounded on three sides by DPR armed formations to the west and south, and the armed formations of the Luhansk People's Republic to the east. The Ukrainian armed forces were still also in control of some of the smaller outlying towns around Debaltseve, including Vuhlehirsk to the southwest. This salient in the Ukrainian armed forces front line not only 'bulged' into DPR-controlled territory, but also as noted now sat astride key communication routes between the DPR and LPR.

On 22 January 2015, the DPR armed formations, including Kalmius and Oplot Brigades, supported by Russian Federation ground forces,[23] began a concerted effort to take control of Debaltseve. These forces included elements from the DPR's Kalmius and Oplot Brigades, organised into a strike group called 'Gorlovka',[24] reportedly comprising 2,000 soldiers and over 20 tanks.[25]

In a particularly well-coordinated campaign, they were assisted by the armed formations of the Luhansk People's Republic who attacked Debaltseve from the eastern side. In addition, mercenaries and armoured vehicles from the Russian private military company Wagner Group were also involved, in probably the most high-profile involvement of that organisation in eastern Ukraine until 2022.[26] Numerous modern Russian Federation military vehicles were identified in the battle for Debaltseve, including the BPM-97 Vystrel and GAZ Vodnik, as well as advanced models of T-72 tanks with their insignia obscured.

Heavy artillery fire targeted Ukrainian armed forces positions in and around Debaltseve, and the M03 highway, the main route leading out of Debaltseve to Ukrainian positions in Luhanske to the northwest was dangerously open and exposed. Despite having constructed dense fortifications and defensive positions in and around Debaltseve, coordinated attacks on three sides by DPR, LPR, and Russian forces eventually forced the Ukrainian armed forces to retreat, with the remaining forces escaping north along the M03 highway to avoid being totally encircled.

Heavy artillery fire caused significant casualties among both the Ukrainian armed forces defending Debaltseve, as well as the civilian population. As one analyst of the battle wrote at the time, 'the battle that raged in and around the city of Debaltseve has only a few comparisons in scale and intensity in post-war European history, notably being Sarajevo and Grozny.'[27]

Fierce fighting continued in Debaltseve despite the signing of the Minsk II agreement on 12 February 2015, which aimed at stopping the fighting in Donbas.[28] Zakharchenko, who reportedly considered the Minsk Agreements a 'betrayal,' claimed that the Minsk II agreement did not apply to Debaltseve in order to keep his forces engaged. On 18 February 2015, Debaltseve was finally captured by combined DPR, LPR and Russian ground forces.

Minsk II and Reorganisation of DPR Armed Formations

After the DPR capture of Debaltseve and the signing of Minsk II, there was a concerted effort by the Kremlin to reorganise the DPR and LPR's armed formations. As Minsk II called for the eventual reintegration of the DPR and LPR back into Ukraine under a new decentralised system, there was a recognition among the DPR's Russian curators that the unruly and violent battalions of 2014 would have to be reshaped into something more able to participate in the functioning of a state.

This involved reigning in the more extreme unit commanders, in particular the ones who opposed the Minsk Agreements, and trying to end the destructive internecine warfare between factions within the two People's Republics.

This process was marginally easier in the DPR, which – largely thanks to Girkin's initial actions – had retained a more united command structure. Unlike the LPR, where this process was accompanied by numerous violent targeted assassinations, in the DPR the removal or side-lining of commanders who had fallen out of favour was more or less orderly. The DPR's units were arranged into the DPR 1st Army Corps. Vladimir Kononov had taken over as Defence Minister after Igor Girkin's resignation.

КОНОНОВ
ВЛАДИМИР
ПЕТРОВИЧ

Vladimir Kononov, DPR Defence Minister. Postcard no. 3 in the set 'Gold Star Heroes', issued by the DPR Ministry of Communication, 2017. (Author's collection)

Minsk II called for withdrawal of heavy weapons by both sides beyond agreed lines depending on the capability of the weapons system. Neither side fully implemented this, and there were disagreements about where the withdrawal lines were, as Minsk II had been drawn up while the Debaltseve battle was still ongoing, so the 'bulge' of the Ukrainian lines around Debaltseve was reflected in the withdrawal lines. This became something the DPR did not agree with later on, as it meant their withdrawal lines were much further back than 'facts on the ground' dictated.

'Frozen' Conflict (February 2015 – February 2022)

The DPR capture of the Debaltseve salient in early 2015 represented the last major change in the front line between the Ukrainian armed forces and the DPR armed formations until 2022. After the capture of Debaltseve, both sides settled down for seven years, with the conflict occurring across the so-called 'contact line' between the two sides.

Running for approximately 250km in Donetsk oblast, the contact line started in the north on the border with Luhansk oblast just north of Debaltseve and ran west towards and around Horlivka, which the DPR controlled, then turned southwest towards Donetsk. Here it

Image of Vostok Battalion flag on hill at Savur-Mohyla. This 270-metre high position was bitterly contested in the summer of 2014. (Photograph by Dean O'Brien)

terricones allowed the DPR to position forward observers to direct artillery fire.

Trenches were constructed by hand in frontline areas, and often revetted with wooden planking or corrugated iron to prevent their collapse. Fall back positions in rear areas – where construction could be undertaken without fear of drawing Ukrainian fire – were sometimes constructed using mechanical means, such as the EOV-4421 or Soviet-era TMK trench digger. In less active or less strategically important sectors, such as on the eastern banks of the Kalmius River, the DPR constructed strongpoints modelled on the Soviet pattern, formed of trenches and vehicle revetments in wide ovals or squares, usually on high ground which commanded the surrounding area.

Given the length of the contact line under DPR control, around 250km, it was not possible for the DPR to occupy any more than relatively small sections of the contact line with significant numbers of militants for long periods of time. After the withdrawal of the majority of Russian Federation ground forces after the capture of Debaltseve in 2015, the DPR broadly employed a strategy of occupying its frontline positions where possible with small, platoon-sized forces whose task was to act as 'tripwires' to warn of any impending assault by the Ukrainian armed forces. When there was escalation of fighting in a particular sector, the necessary DPR forces would be rushed to the location to engage in the fighting.

In some ways this mirrored the DPR's wider military strategy. As the Ukrainian military rebuilt itself and rapidly developed its capabilities after 2014, it soon reached a point where it possessed military superiority over the armed formations of the DPR and LPR. As well as simply being able to call on a far greater population and economic base, Ukraine possessed advantages in military airpower and other key areas. However, the constant presence of significant Russian forces from the Southern Military District over the border acted as an implied 'security guarantee' for the DPR. In the case of a surprise Ukrainian assault, the armed formations of the DPR would buy time for reinforcements to arrive from Russia.

Various 'flashpoints' came to the fore during the years from 2015 to 2022. These tended to be in areas where the Ukrainian armed forces and DPR armed formations were particularly close to each other. Some flashpoints – measured by the number of Minsk ceasefire violations recorded by the international observer mission and the respective JCCC officers – became prominent for a short period of time, others, like the Avdiivka-Yasynuvata axis, remained 'hot' for many years.

ran close to the E50 highway, which fell on the DPR-controlled side of the line. The line encompassed Yasynuvata, an important railway junction, and then cut across the shattered remains of Donetsk International Airport. From here, the line turned south and encompassed most of the urban areas of Donetsk, Staromykhailivka was under DPR control, as was Oleksandrivka to the south, both western outliers of Donetsk city. The line then curved southeast around Donetsk, Olenivka and Dokuchaievsk were both frontline DPR communities. It then ran just south of the small village of Petrivske. Further southeast, the line ran along the length of the Kalmius River which provided a natural barrier between the two sides, with most of the bridges across it destroyed. The Ukrainian armed forces had recaptured the small town of Pavlopil, so here the line diverted from the Kalmius River and went almost straight south towards the Azov Sea, bulging a little to encompass the small village of Pikuzy, and finally ending on the shores of the Azov Sea just east of Shyrokyne.

In this mostly static form of warfare, the DPR dug many miles of trenches and built extensive fortifications, and observers of the conflict during this period often made comparisons to the First World War. In more important and 'hot spot' active sectors, such as around Yasynuvata and Oleksandrivka west of Donetsk, the DPR's trenches were effectively contiguous for many miles, with frontline trenches and bunkers connected to communication trenches leading to rearward areas.

The Donbas as a whole is mostly flat and featureless, and the hill at Savur-Mohyla, so bitterly contested in 2014, was the highest point in the region at a modest 270m. However, other important heights were fought over, these being man-made mine spoil heaps, known locally as 'terricones'. Left over from centuries of mining activity in the area, some of these conical artificial hills became important tactical positions for the DPR, allowing them to command the surrounding area. Small fortified dugouts on the top of these

Trade and Economics

Another important aspect of the conflict in Donbas was that the contact line was never completely sealed off. Various major crossing

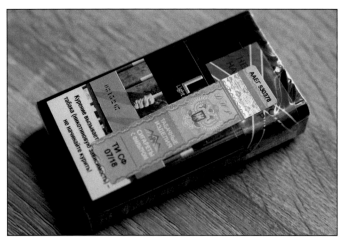

Control of the lucrative trade in cigarettes was thought to be behind the enrichment of certain DPR leaders, and reason behind some of the infighting seen within the two People's Republics. Beneath the DPR tax sticker is a second sticker, marked with the Novorossiya flag, which notes that the cigarettes are not to be sold on the territory of the Russian Federation. Tax sticker dated to July 2018. (Author's collection)

Another example of a Novorossiya cigarette pack. (Photograph by Dean O'Brien)

points had to remain open, to allow people to cross backwards and forwards. Many people who remained in the DPR and LPR-controlled parts of Donbas had families and lives that straddled the line of contact, and pensioners on the NGCA side had to cross into Ukrainian-controlled areas to collect their pensions.

These crossing points became scenes of great suffering for the civilian population, with thousands of people queuing for hours in the freezing temperatures of winter or the baking heat of summer, as documents were checked by both sides and baggage searched. These checkpoints had to be staffed, usually by armed members from the DPR's Ministry of State Security (MGB), as well as units from the respective armed formation in control of the section of the contact line under which the checkpoint came. Such units would often lay landmines to secure their positions in the verges on each side of the roads that crossed towards the Ukrainian side, and as a result many civilian casualties occurred.

In Donetsk there were three major crossing points, at Maiorsk northwest of Horlivka, Oleksandrivka west of Donetsk, and Olenivka to the southwest of Donetsk. Bizarrely, there was even a 'duty free' kiosk in the Grey Zone at the DPR checkpoint at Olenivka, allowing purchase of cigarettes and alcohol, situated just in front of a marked minefield.[29]

In addition to the crossing points for people, cross-border flows of freight continued, with coal trains continuing to make the crossing over the contact line until as late as 2017. This was owing to the nature of the large oligarch-owned heavy industrial concerns which owned multiple facilities across the Donbas, and who negotiated access and continued operation with the DPR. It was only in early 2017 when this trade

over the contact line was finally stopped by Ukrainian volunteer battalions who blockaded railway lines and roads.[30]

With its out-of-date factories and declining coal industry, population loss owing to people fleeing the region, plus the damage inflicted to major infrastructure by the conflict, the DPR was never anything but a massive financial drain on the coffers of its patron, the Russian Federation. Some researchers highlighted the '...significant cost of keeping the 'People's Republics' afloat. Russia's non-military subsidies for the 'People's Republics' are thought to amount to €2 billion per year, almost one percent of Russia's federal budget'.[31]

This was in part owing to the interlocking nature of the economy of the Donbas. Though the DPR had control of major industrial centres like Donetsk and Horlivka, it had not taken control of the massive coking plant at Avdiivka, or the port and gigantic metal

'Humanitarian Aid from the Russian Federation'. A monument dedicated to the Russian Federation's State Emergency Services (MChS), near the town of Amrosiivka. In reality, Russian aid was modest in comparison to the massive scale of the humanitarian and economic problems faced by people living in the non-government-controlled areas of the DPR and LPR. Amrosiivka, February 2017. (Private photo collection, used with permission)

factories in Mariupol, upon which those industrial centres depended. As the eminent British strategist Lawrence Freedman noted '...the position reached in early September [2014] was not naturally stable. Having separatists occupy ... territory undoubtedly created a serious problem for Ukraine, but the amount held was not enough to advance Russia's original objectives. At about 7 percent of Ukraine's total it was too small to make much sense as a stand-alone entity, incoherent both economically and politically'.[32]

Trade was continued with the Russian Federation, controlled by a shadowy organisation called Vneshtorgservis. This organisation was registered in the similarly Russian-backed unrecognised state of South Ossetia, which offered Russia a

This photograph shows the interior of a heavily fortified DPR position in Yasynuvata. The soldier carries an AK-74 rifle. (Photograph by Dean O'Brien)

flimsy fig leaf of non-involvement. Vneshtorgservis, a company with almost zero online presence, was a way for Russia to funnel financial support to the DPR and LPR without being directly involved.

Trade was mainly in coal from those mines still operating, carried east across the border by rail from the DPR into the Russian Federation. However, a leaked letter written to Denis Pushilin brought to light a desperate and exploitative position for those coal mines operating under DPR control, in which '...the situation is critical due to delayed payments for coal delivered to OAO Vneshtorgservis and its subsidiary Ugol Donbassa [...] As of June 3, 2019, RUB 1,586.6 million was outstanding, of which RUB 962.1mn was overdue'.[33]

Changes to the Contact Line

Small changes occurred in the shape of the contact line after the DPR capture of Debaltseve. In the far south, the small town of Shyrokyne on the shores of the Azov Sea, some 10km east of Mariupol, became the scene of intense fighting between the DPR armed formations – most likely elements of the 9th Mariupol-Khingan Regiment – and the Ukrainian armed forces. Control of the town swayed between one side and the other until February 2016, when the DPR withdrew from their positions in the town, pulling back eastwards to a defensive line some 2km away. The town itself suffered massive damage during the fighting and was almost completely abandoned.

In late January 2017, the DPR launched an offensive against the Ukrainian-controlled town of Avdiivka, a large industrial town close to the front lines, across from DPR positions at Yasynuvata. Vostok Regiment and Somalia Battalion were the principle DPR units involved in this offensive. The battle lasted several days, with intense artillery bombardment and a tank attack by the DPR. It has been suggested that the Kremlin did not approve of this offensive and refused to provide further support as the fighting intensified. By 4 Feb 2017 the battle was over, with the DPR having withdrawn to its previous positions, and the Ukrainian armed forces having made some small territorial gains.

Another feature of the initial front lines that solidified after the battle for Debaltseve was that there was often a significant stand-off distance between the opposing sides. The so-called 'Grey Zone' in between the lines was in some cases quite substantial, in some cases measuring several kilometres depending on the terrain and other geographical features. In places, whole villages were left stranded in this 'No Man's Land' with neither side exercising complete control over them.

Over the subsequent years, both sides made inroads into this 'Grey Zone', slowly incorporating territory and pushing trenches and defensive positions further forwards. The tiny village of Pikuzy (formerly Kominternove), some 12km northeast of Mariupol, was in this manner occupied by DPR forces in December 2015, having formerly been located in the Grey Zone.[34]

In some cases, this erosion of the 'Grey Zone' between the Ukrainian armed forces positions and those of the DPR armed formations resulted in very close proximity between the two sides. As an example, northwest of Yasynuvata, a DPR-controlled railway junction north of Donetsk, by 2018 defensive positions occupied by the Vostok Regiment were situated some 250m away from the closest Ukrainian armed forces positions to the northwest. This close proximity was a contributing factor to intense bouts of fighting.

Joint Centre for Control and Coordination

The Joint Centre for Control and Coordination (JCCC, or СЦКК in both Russian and Ukrainian) was an organisation comprising both Ukrainian and Russian military officers, which was set up in 2014. The organisation's purpose was to monitor the Minsk ceasefire agreement.

Moreover, the Russian officers in the JCCC were also able to exert some – but never total – control over the DPR armed formation units within their sector, enabling localised ceasefires for infrastructure repair or the passage of civilians across the contact line. Vast Soviet-era infrastructure including power lines and water pipes crossed the

Logo worn by the self-appointed DPR 'JCCC' officers, who took over 'cooperation' duties on the NGCA after the departure of the remaining Russian Federation JCCC officers in December 2017. (Logo image in the public domain)

'He was a president of the battlefield.' Magnet commemorating Aleksander Zakharchenko, c. 2019. (Author's collection)

Stamp and first day envelope commemorating the inauguration of Denis Pushilin as Head of the DPR. Stamp and envelope issued 20th November 2018. (Author's collection)

contact line at various places and proved hard and expensive for either side to 'isolate.'

The Donetsk Water Filtration Station, for example, provided clean water to both Ukrainian and DPR-controlled areas. It was situated in the 'Grey Zone' between the frontline positions of both sides in the Avdiivka-Yasynuvata hotspot, but its brave civilian staff kept it operating in order to provide potable water to thousands of people. When fighting damaged the Station's infrastructure or the pipes taking water in or out, cooperation was needed to get the water flowing again.

For a while, groups of Ukrainian and Russian officers were situated at various locations on both sides of the contact line, however as time went on the Ukrainian officers were deployed to fewer locations in the NGCA owing to fears for their safety, leaving only Russian officers on the NGCA side.

Eventually in December 2017 Russia withdrew its officers from the JCCC completely, effectively ceasing this form of cooperation. However, cross-contact line 'cooperation' was still sometimes required, and a few DPR armed formation officers were informally badged as 'JCCC' to continue some of the functions performed by the Russian officers previously.

Such officers wore large brassards marked with a DPR 'JCCC' logo, which included three crossed swords. Owing to Ukraine's lack of recognition of the DPR, such officers never had any formal recognition by the Ukrainian side.

Assassination of Zakharchenko (August 2018)

On 31 August 2018, Aleksandr Zakharchenko was killed by a bomb explosion in central Donetsk. The blast took place at the 'Separ' Café – the name derived from the word 'separatist' – which was a military-themed café on Donetsk's Pushkin Boulevard, replete with camouflage décor and a display of weapons and ammunition. The bomb had been placed in the café before Zakharchenko's arrival and was detonated shortly after he entered the restaurant.

The DPR was quick to blame the Ukrainian SBU and/or unnamed Western intelligence agencies, and though this cannot be ruled out

Denis Pushilin (with beard) on Republic Day. (Photograph by Dean O'Brien)

A shrine to Aleksandr Zakharchenko, killed by a bomb explosion at the 'Separ' Café in central Donetsk. (Photograph by Dean O'Brien)

After a brief interregnum, Denis Pushilin took over as head of the DPR. Pushilin had been prominent in the DPR leadership in 2014 before being sidelined by Zakharchenko. Notably, in comparison to Zakharchenko, Pushilin had always been in favour of the DPR joining the Russian Federation rather than becoming an independent state.

After Zakharchenko's death, there was further reorganisation and centralisation of the DPR's armed formations. The DPR Ministry of Defence was abolished in September 2018, with all armed formation units transferred to the DPR 1st Army Corps or the Ministry of Internal Affairs.[35] Nominally the abolition was because there was no provision for a DPR Ministry of Defence under the Minsk Agreements, but it was likely owing to a desire to curb the unwelcome growing

entirely, it is thought far more likely that Zakharchenko was killed either by a rival faction within the DPR, or because he had started to become too 'independent' for the Kremlin.

independence of certain DPR units, and indeed the DPR more broadly under Zakharchenko.

6
COMMAND AND CONTROL OF DPR 1st ARMY CORPS

The armed formations of the DPR relied heavily on military, logistical and political support from the Russian Federation. At the political level, the emerging leaders of the DPR relied heavily on support from powerful figures in the Kremlin, so-called 'Curators' who advised and pushed DPR agendas within the Kremlin.

The Russian academic Medvedev noted that senior members of the DPR leadership were rumoured to meet with Kremlin figures '… in Moscow, in a separate room in the 'Kofemaniya' café on Bolshoi Cherkassy Lane, exactly half way between the FSB building on Lubyanka Square and the Presidential Administration headquarters on Staraya Square. Alexander Borodai, ministers from the DPR and senior representatives of the Presidential Administration have been spotted there.'[1]

On a military level, some Ukrainian sources claimed that the DPR 1st Army Corps and LPR 2nd Army Corps were directly controlled as subordinate units within the 8th Army of the Russian Federation's Southern Military District.[2] Other research supported this 'direct control' theory, suggesting that: 'The rebel armed forces in eastern Ukraine are regarded as reserve formations of the Russian Armed Forces (probably at the formal rank of auxiliary territorial defence troops in order to differentiate them from regular Russian troops).'[3]

In this view, while the lower ranks were staffed by 'Donbas locals', the vast majority of staff and command positions within the DPR armed formations were occupied by up to 2,000 senior officers from the Russian Armed Forces, who were posted on a rotational basis.[4]

This viewpoint was broadly shared by most Western observers, who noted the importance of the Southern Military District to Kremlin military planning, and examined the ways in which the Southern Military District provided support to the armed formations of the DPR and LPR.[5]

The idea that the armed formations of the DPR were a formal extension of Russian forces also suited the Ukrainian narrative which framed the conflict as an international one. In this way the DPR armed formations (as well as those of the neighbouring LPR) were commonly described by the Ukrainian government and military as the 'occupying forces of the Russian Federation in the Donbas' (In Ukrainian: Окупаційні війська РФ на Донбасі).

This position was central to Ukraine's strategy since the beginning of the conflict in 2014, which sought to place blame for the conflict on Russia as an aggressor country. As a result, Ukraine steadfastly refused to directly negotiate with representatives from the DPR and LPR, for a fear of potentially being seen to give them legitimacy.

This central tenet of Ukrainian policy was further enshrined in the legal system, such as the 2018 law "On the state policy to ensure the state sovereignty of Ukraine in the temporarily occupied territories in Donetsk and Luhansk regions." This law firmly framed Russia as the aggressor country, temporarily occupying the Donetsk and Luhansk NGCAs, and therefore precluded any ceding of 'authority' by Ukraine to the DPR and LPR.[6]

Failure of the Novorossiya Project

However, irrespective of the perception of the DPR 1st Army Corps as a formal extension of Russian Southern Military District, it is evident that the units of the DPR 1st Army Corps – and indeed the DPR as an entity more broadly – enjoyed a certain autonomy. It is exactly the nature of this autonomy, and the nature of the proxy-benefactor relationship, which is worth examining.

Within the DPR's armed formations, a fractious and often bitter relationship between the key commanders and units was evident from the start. Igor Girkin attempted to improve this coordination when he arrived in Donetsk after the withdrawal from Sloviansk: 'A Military Council was founded by Strelkov in an attempt to unite the main DNR groups whose members included Strelkov, his chief of staff *Mikhailo*, Mozgovoi from LNR, Khmuryi … and Bezler, but Zakharchenko, the commander of the *Oplot*, was present only twice and Khodakovsky of *Vostok* did not wish to conduct joint operations with them at all.'[7]

However, despite this and probably because of Girkin's attempts, the DPR managed to retain a more unified command and control structure than the armed formations of the neighbouring LPR.

In terms of relations between the DPR and LPR, the relatively early and publicly announced failure of the 'Novorossiya Project' exposed the differences between the de facto authorities of the two regions. Announced in May 2014 as a confederation of the two areas, less than a year later it was announced that the political project would be cancelled, and the DPR and LPR remained as two distinct entities. As a result, the initial plan to create a joint military structure covering the two areas, the United Armed Forces of Novorossiya, also foundered.

While various theories have been put forwards for the failure of the Novorossiya confederation, including pressure from Russia,[8] one of the main reasons is likely to have been the infighting and opaque power politics being played out within the DPR and LPR.[9]

As a result, the failure to unite the DPR and LPR into a larger political structure also led to the creation of two army corps to match these two entities,[10] the 1st Army Corps for the DPR and the 2nd Army Corps for the LPR.

The failure of the Novorossiya confederation project and process of the creation of the two army corps casts a different light on the 'total control' supposedly exercised over DPR 1st Army Corps by Russia, and more broadly on the nature of the proxy-benefactor relationship between the Russian Federation and the DPR/LPR in eastern Ukraine.

Simply put, Russian control over the DPR and LPR had its limits. 'Foreign Minister Sergei Lavrov acknowledged Moscow's influence with the separatists, but he also insisted that it was not "as great as 100 percent." Separatist leaders asserted their wish to be wholly independent of Ukraine and preferably part of Russia, even though the Minsk agreements gave no support for these possibilities.'[11]

7

DPR 1st ARMY CORPS AND PRINCIPAL UNITS

DPR 1st Army Corps was officially formed on 12 November 2014, unit number 00100, headquartered in Donetsk. This section will provide a brief overview of the principal DPR 1st Army Corps units after the Corp's creation in 2014, including those – like Republican Guard – that joined 1st Army Corps only after Zakharchenko's assassination in 2018.

According to some Ukrainian sources, at some point in 2016 the 1st Army Corps was renamed the "Operational-Tactical Command "Donetsk" of the DPR Ministry of Defence."[1] However, the use of the term 1st Army Corps continued within the DPR after 2016, more frequently than (though sometimes interchangeable with) the term "Operational-Tactical Command Donetsk."

Other Ukrainian analysts later detected a change in terminology after the inauguration of Denis Pushilin in late 2018, and the subsequent abolition of the DPR Ministry of Defence. More emphasis was then placed on the term 'People's Militia' than 'Army Corps', with this change in terminology supposedly designed to make the armed formations of the DPR more 'acceptable' within the framework of the Minsk Agreements, by which the DPR would be absorbed back into Ukraine.[2]

However, these linguistic changes did not alter the fact that the DPR 1st Army Corps existed within the area controlled by the DPR, and had a fairly well-defined structure that changed as units were added or removed. For this reason, the book will refer to DPR 1st

Army Corps as the overall umbrella unit for the vast majority of the DPR's frontline military strength, despite these possible 'cosmetic' changes to its nomenclature.

This section will try and list notable sub-units, in particular 'named' units, however these – and indeed the estimates of total strength – should be read with caution owing to the seemingly constant reorganisation and transfer of units within the DPR during this period, and the concomitant lack of solid information on unit strength and composition.

As one astute observer of the conflict noted in 2016, there was '…a certain amount of exaggeration and "inflation" regarding the DPR's structure … However, there are no official figures to go by, and, with a very out-of-date official website, it is impossible to get a real sense of size, number and structure.'[3] In 2016, Ukrainian estimates put the total strength of DPR 1st Army Corps at 20,000 people, compared to just under 15,000 for the LPR 2nd Army Corps.[4]

Tactical Symbols

One interesting area of open source research was that tracking the evolving unit symbology used by DPR 1st Army Corps units. This was especially useful in trying to track vehicles and units on social media.

Early tactical symbols were quite diverse, comprising rhomboids or diamonds with numbers or symbols inside. By late 2018, DPR 1st

DPR 1st Army Corps insignia. Full colour patch, c. 2016. (Author's collection)

Table 1: Known tactical markings of DPR 1st Army Corps units

Unit type	Unit name	Assigned number
Brigade ▲	1 Slavyansk	51
	3 Berkut	53
	5 Oplot	55
	100 Republican Guard	50
	Separate Artillery Brigade Kalmius	13
Regiment ■	9th Mariupol-Khingan Separate Motorised Rifle Regiment	59
	11th Separate Enakievo-Danube Motorised Rifle Regiment "Vostok"	61
	Separate Commandant's Regiment	29
Battalion ●	2nd Separate Tank Battalion "Diesel"	19
	10th Separate Special Operations Battalion "Khan"	31 and/or 27
	Separate Repair Battalion "Kongo"	33
	Battalion of Command and Guard	15

Army Corps units appeared to have settled on a fairly simple system which used triangles for brigades, squares for regiments, and circles for battalions. Numbers inside these shapes denoted the actual unit.

DPR Ministry of Defence insignia. Subdued patch, c. 2016. (Author's collection)

Table 1 only shows those units for which unit symbols and numbers are known.

It has been observed that brigades belonging to the DPR 1st Army Corps were generally assigned odd numbers, and those belonging to the LPR 2nd Army Corps were assigned even numbers.[5]

1st Separate Slavyansk Motorised Rifle Brigade (1-я Отдельная Славянская Мотострелковая Бригада)

Slavyansk Brigade's genesis was in the fighting in and around Sloviansk in 2014, during which time DPR forces were commanded by Igor Strelkin. At the core of the unit were around 50 fighters of the 'Crimea Company' recruited in Crimea, who crossed the border and ignited the fighting.

These men were augmented by around 300 – 350 local fighters from the area around Sloviansk,[8] but after the withdrawal from Sloviansk on 5 July 2014 the unit underwent several reorganisations, in which it merged with other units, eventually coalescing into the First Slavyansk Brigade. When the DPR's military units were later structured into the DPR 1st Army Corps, the First Slavyansk Brigade became the First Separate Slavyansk Motorised Rifle Brigade.

For a short period of time in 2015, part of the Girkin's Slavyansk Brigade was formed into the DPR 1st Army Corps 7th Slavyansk Motorised Rifle Brigade (unit number 08807). This brigade had at least one motorised rifle battalion. At an unknown date, probably in mid to late 2015, the 7th Slavyansk Motorised Rifle Brigade was transferred to the LPR 2nd Army Corps, and disappeared from the DPR 1st Army Corps.

The First Separate Slavyansk Motorised Rifle Brigade was headquartered in Kalmiuske (formerly Komsomolske), in the southern part of the Donetsk oblast NGCA. One of the first DPR units to be reorganised along the lines of a Russian motorised rifle brigade, Slavyansk reportedly included four tank companies equipped with T-72 and T-64 main battle tanks, totalling around 40 tanks.[9]

One of the original units in Slavyansk was the Konstantinovka[10] Battalion, which fought at numerous hotspots in the first year of the conflict.[11] Later it became a reconnaissance battalion in Slavyansk. Also in Slavyansk was a motorised rifle battalion called "Viking," with several companies equipped with BMP-1 and BMP-2 infantry fighting vehicles, and MT-LBs.

Estimates of total strength for the brigade ranged from around 3,500 to 4,500 personnel.

3rd Separate Motorised Rifle Brigade "Berkut" (3-я Отдельная Мотострелковая Бригада «Беркут»)

Berkut solidified from the so-called 'Bezler Group' which battled Ukrainian forces for control of the important city of Horlivka in 2014. Reportedly initially comprising of just 20 people, at its inception, the Bezler Group was commanded by the eponymous Igor Bezler, call sign 'Bes' (Demon). He had formerly been a Lieutenant Colonel in the Russian Armed Forces, and the Ukrainian SBU alleged he was in the employ of the Russian GRU when the conflict in Donbas started.

1st Slavyansk insignia. Full colour patch, c. 2018. (Author's collection)

1st Slavyansk Battalion, 7th Motorised Rifle Battalion insignia. Subdued patch, c. 2015. This unit was transferred in 2015 to the LPR 2nd Army Corps. (Author's collection)

In the very early stages of the conflict, Bezler and his first fighters appear to have worked alongside Strelkov in the battle for Sloviansk in 2014. However, after some violent disagreement or friction, they left and moved to the city of Horlivka, where Bezler had been working before the conflict.

In Horlivka, the '…rebel campaign was marred by egregious acts of violence, arbitrary killings, hostage-taking, kidnapping (particularly of women), beatings and generalised intimidation. Igor Bezler, known as 'the Demon,' was one of the most feared and brutal of the insurgent leaders … using his headquarters in Gorlovka to dispense summary "justice."'[12]

After helping to seize Horlivka from Ukrainian forces, by many accounts Berkut remained a more autonomous unit than the other key DPR brigades, despite eventual absorption into DPR 1st Army Corps. This is probably because of the hostility Bezler publicly

Troops of the 3rd Separate Motorised Rifle Brigade "Berkut" at the May 2019 Victory Day Parade. (Photograph by Dean O'Brien)

Type of unit	Name of unit	Unit number	HQ (if known)	Composition
Brigade	1st Separate Slavyansk Motorised Rifle Brigade	08801	Kalmiuske	Tank battalion
				1st motorised rifle battalion "Viking"
				2nd motorised rifle battalion "Slavyansk"
				3rd motorised rifle battalion
				Reconnaissance battalion "Konstantinovka"
	3rd Separate Motorised Rifle Brigade "Berkut"	08803	Horlivka	Tank battalion
				2nd motorised rifle battalion
				3rd motorised rifle battalion "Mech"[6]
				Howitzer artillery battalion
				Rocket artillery battalion "Corsa"
				Self-propelled artillery battalion
	5th Separate Motorised Rifle Brigade "Oplot"	08805	Donetsk	Tank battalion
				2nd motorised rifle battalion
				3rd motorised rifle battalion
				Howitzer artillery battalion
				Rocket artillery battalion
				Self-propelled artillery battalion
				Anti-aircraft missile battalion
	100th Separate Motorised Rifle Brigade "Republican Guard"	08826	Donetsk	1st battalion tactical group
				2nd battalion tactical group "Oplot"
				3rd battalion tactical group
				4th battalion tactical group "Cheburashka"
				5th battalion tactical group "Varyag"
				6th battalion tactical group
				7th battalion tactical group
				8th battalion tactical group "Pyatnashka"
				9th battalion tactical group
				"Patriot" Company
				"Viking" Company
				Separate battalion of special purpose
	Separate Artillery Brigade "Kalmius"	08802	Donetsk	Reconnaissance battalion
				1st artillery battalion
				2nd artillery battalion Anti-tank divizion[7]
				Howitzer artillery battalion
				Self-propelled artillery battalion

Table 2: Known units of DPR 1st Army Corps

displayed towards the senior DPR leadership in Donetsk, reportedly once including a violent failed attempt to seize power in Donetsk.[13]

Berkut (Russian for 'Golden Eagle') maintained a lower profile on social media than other DPR units,[14] making it harder to assess

Table 2: Known units of DPR 1st Army Corps (*continued*)

Regiment	9th Mariupol-Khingan Separate Motorised Rifle Regiment	08819	Novoazovsk	Tank battalion
				2nd motorised rifle battalion
				3rd motorised rifle battalion
				Self-propelled artillery divizion
				Howitzer artillery divizion
	11th Separate Enakievo-Danube Motorised Rifle Regiment "Vostok"	08818	Makiivka	Tank battalion
				1st motorised rifle battalion
				2nd motorised rifle battalion
				Self-propelled artillery battalion
				Howitzer artillery battalion
				Rocket artillery battalion
				Anti-aircraft missile battalion
	Special Purpose Regiment of the DPR Ministry of Defence	02707	Donetsk (?)	Chechen battalion
				Pyatnashka battalion
				Patriot battalion
				Prilepin battalion
	Separate Commandant's Regiment	08816	Donetsk	
Battalion	Separate Reconnaissance Battalion "Sparta"	08806	Donetsk	1st reconnaissance company
				2nd reconnaissance company
				3rd reconnaissance company
				Communications platoon
	1st Separate Tank Battalion "Somalia"	08828	Donetsk	1st motorised rifle company
				2nd motorised rifle company
				3rd motorised rifle company
				4th tank company
	2nd Separate Tank Battalion "Diesel"	08810	Donetsk	1st tank company
				2nd tank company
				3rd tank company
				4th tank company
				5th motorised rifle company
				Artillery divizion
	10th Separate Special Operations Battalion "Khan"	08808	Donetsk	1st Special Operations Company 'Essence of Time'
	Separate Repair Battalion "Congo"	08813	Donetsk	
	Separate Battalion of Command and Guard	08804 (?)	Donetsk	

its overall capability, and was notably always absent from the 9 May Victory Day parades held in central Donetsk.

In November 2014, Bezler was 'retired' from control of the Bezler Group and went into exile in Crimea, and the unit was absorbed into the DPR 1st Army Corps as the Third Separate Motorised Rifle Brigade 'Berkut.' According to some sources, as well as the remnants of the original Bezler Group, reportedly coal miners from Horlivka

Poster for Corsa Battalion. The text along the bottom reads: 'I am Russian – And proud of it!' Poster, c. 2016. (Private photo collection, used with permission)

Oplot insignia. Full colour patch, c. 2018. (Author's collection)

Poster advertising the Oplot TV channel. Donetsk, 2018. (Private photo collection, used with permission)

Republican Guard insignia. Late pattern, full colour, c. 2018. The hammer in hand at centre is adapted from the Donetsk city shield. (Author's collection)

and surrounding cities as well as former members of the Ukrainian MVD and SBU,[15] Berkut included volunteers from Crimea.

Headquartered in Horlivka, in the northern part of the Donetsk oblast NGCA, Berkut was deployed along a section of contact line running from the village of Pantelemonivka in the south, the northwards around the western and northern sides of the city of Horlivka.

On its eastern flank, the remainder of the contact line within Donetsk oblast was held by the LPR 7th Separate Motorised Rifle Brigade. Though geographically situated within the boundaries of Donetsk oblast, and falling under the control of the DPR in terms of civilian administration, the armed formations stationed in Debaltseve were those of the 7th Separate Motorised Rifle Brigade of the LPR 2nd Army Corps. The LPR 7th Brigade was also positioned in several smaller towns and villages to the west of Debaltseve, where its area of responsibility abutted that of Berkut.

Berkut's strength included four tank companies equipped with T-72 and T-64BV main battle tanks, as well as motorised rifle companies equipped with BMP-1 infantry fighting vehicles. Artillery systems included the 122mm D-30 towed and 2S1 Gvozdika self-propelled artillery pieces. There was also a battalion of rocket artillery, called the Corsa Battalion, equipped with BM-21 Grad multiple launch rocket systems.[16] Estimates of strength for this brigade varied widely from 1,000 to 4,500 personnel.

Berkut's 'golden eagle' insignia was almost identical to that of the pre-Maidan Ukrainian Berkut riot police unit which was disbanded after the fall of Yanukovych. The yellow and blue background of the riot police was replaced in the DPR Berkut insignia with the colours of the Russian flag. The identical name and highly similar insignia is most likely explained by the prevalence of members of the Ukrainian Ministry of Internal Affairs who defected in 2014 to the small units which later coalesced into the DPR's Berkut Brigade.

5th Separate Motorised Rifle Brigade "Oplot" (5-я Отдельная Мотострелковая Бригада «Оплот»)

The Fifth Separate Motorised Rifle Brigade "Oplot" (Russian for 'Bastion' or 'Stronghold') is interesting and unusual among the main DPR brigades in that it had an organisational history prior to the start of the Ukrainian conflict in 2014.

Oplot was founded as a public organisation in Kharkiv in 2010 by Evgeny Zhilin, a former officer of the Ukrainian Ministry of Internal Affairs. His parents had worked at the famous Malyshev tank factory in Kharkiv, where the Ukrainian T-84 Oplot main battle tank was developed after the collapse of the Soviet Union, and apparently this led him to choose the name 'Oplot' for his organisation, in honour of his parents.[17]

Among various activities, Oplot had a sports club wing numbering around 350 members, which rose to notoriety in 2014 for its members reportedly being among some of the most violent anti-Maidan fighters.

In 2014, after being unsuccessful in attempts to

Republican Guard soldiers wearing light-blue berets and the striped undershirts (тельняшки/ Telnyashka) associated with Soviet and Russian VDV (airborne) forces, seen here at the Victory Day Parade. (Photograph by Dean O'Brien)

Patriot insignia. Full colour patch, c. 2018. (Author's collection)

Pyatnashka insignia. Full colour patch, c. 2018. (Author's collection)

seize power in Kharkiv,[18] most of the members of the Kharkiv branch of Oplot moved to Donetsk to shore up the power of the nascent DPR there. Twenty members of Oplot were among those who stormed and occupied the Donetsk city council building on 16 April 2014, demanding a referendum be held on the region's future.[19] The leader of the Donetsk branch of Oplot, Alexander Zakharchenko, would later rise to be the leader of the DPR overall, while Evgeny Zhilin was murdered in mysterious circumstances in Russia in 2016.[20]

As with other DPR brigades, after the chaotic early days of the conflict in 2014, the unit was eventually subsumed into the DPR 1st Army Corps as the Fifth Separate Motorised Brigade "Oplot" and retained the organisation's rhino logo in its insignia. In September 2014, Oplot absorbed one of the more prominent early DPR armed formations, the controversial Russian Orthodox Army, which had been implicated in the killing of civilians in Sloviansk.[21]

The Oplot name was also used by the associated DPR TV channel of the same name.[22] The TV channel enjoyed particular prominence during Zakharchenko's reign as head of the DPR, but underwent a rebrand, lack of funding and loss of significance after his death in 2018.

Headquartered in Donetsk, Oplot was deployed in areas around Donetsk city, as well as the parts of the contact line to the south of the city, including Dokuchaievsk. At Dokuchaievsk, its units were positioned on the commanding heights atop large spoil heaps, allowing them to dominate a long section of the contact line.

One of the most heavily armed of the DPR brigades, Oplot included a tank battalion equipped with the usual T-64BV and T-72 tanks, motorised rifle battalions with BMP-1 or 2 infantry fighting vehicles, as well as 2S1 and 2S3 self-propelled artillery, BM-21 Grad MLRS, and 9K35 Strela-10 anti-aircraft systems.[23]

Oplot was widely regarded as one of the largest and best-equipped DPR brigades, with estimates of total strength at around 4,300 – 4,500 people.[24]

Ahrik Avidzba, commander of Pyatnashka. Postcard no. 9 in the set 'Gold Star Heroes', issued by the DPR Ministry of Communication, 2017. (Author's collection)

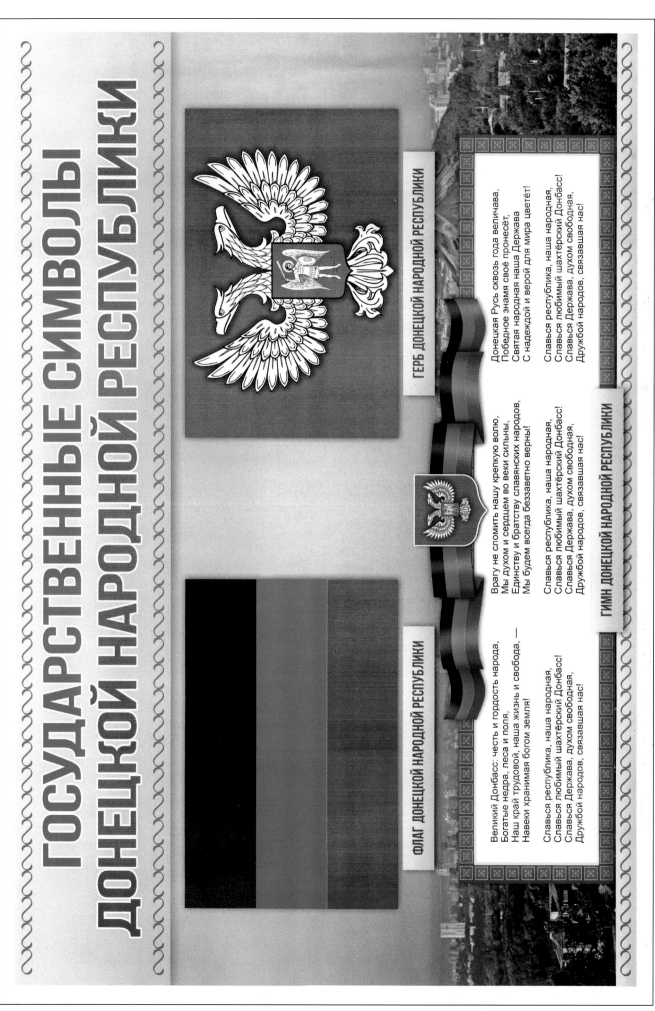

ГОСУДАРСТВЕННЫЕ СИМВОЛЫ
ДОНЕЦКОЙ НАРОДНОЙ РЕСПУБЛИКИ

ГЕРБ ДОНЕЦКОЙ НАРОДНОЙ РЕСПУБЛИКИ

ФЛАГ ДОНЕЦКОЙ НАРОДНОЙ РЕСПУБЛИКИ

ГИМН ДОНЕЦКОЙ НАРОДНОЙ РЕСПУБЛИКИ

Великий Донбасс: честь и гордость народа,
Богатые недра, леса и поля,
Наш край трудовой, наша жизнь и свобода, —
Навеки хранимая богом земля!

Славься республика, наша народная,
Славься любимый шахтёрский Донбасс!
Славься Держава, духом свободная,
Дружбой народов, связавшая нас!

Врагу не сломить нашу крепкую волю,
Мы духом и сердцем во веки сильны,
Единству и братству славянских народов,
Мы будем всегда беззаветно верны!

Славься республика, наша народная,
Славься любимый шахтёрский Донбасс!
Славься Держава, духом свободная,
Дружбой народов, связавшая нас!

Донецкая Русь сквозь года величава,
Победное знамя своё пронесёт,
Святая народная наша Держава
С надеждой и верой для мира цветёт!

Славься республика, наша народная,
Славься любимый шахтёрский Донбасс!
Славься Держава, духом свободная,
Дружбой народов, связавшая нас!

The "official" flag, crest, and national anthem of the DPR para-state. (Author's collection)

The UAZ-23632-148 Esaul was perhaps the most modern vehicle openly supplied to the DPR in the period between 2014 and 2022. Externally almost identical to the civilian UAZ Patriot pickup, the UAZ-23632-148 Esaul was a purpose-built vehicle that incorporated a lot of the lessons learned by the Russian armed forces from improvised 'technicals' used in conflicts in the Middle East. The UAZ Esaul had an armoured cab and engine compartment, as well as protected fuel tanks and other modifications. On the pickup bed was a frame including a ring mount able to take a heavy machine gun or automatic grenade launcher. Fifteen such vehicles were supplied to the DPR in a ceremony in early 2021 attended by Pushilin. (Artwork by David Bocquelet)

Trucks were a highly visible part of the DPR's military activities, especially after the signing of the Minsk agreements when the presence of heavy military equipment near the contact line was proscribed. The DPR had an extensive truck fleet centred around KamAZ variants, such as this KamAZ-4310, and Ural 4x4 and 6x6 variants. (Artwork by David Bocquelet)

The T-64BV was one of the two main types in the DPR tank fleet. This vehicle is depicted as presented during the important 9 May parades in Donetsk, with ceremonial St. George's ribbon down the side, and five-pointed red star. Vehicles on parade were usually painted in uniform dark green, devoid of unit or tactical number markings. (Artwork by David Bocquelet)

The MT-LB performed many roles in the DPR's armed formations, acting as armoured personnel carrier, artillery prime mover, and as an improvised platform for various weapons systems. This vehicle was one used by the DPR in the early stages of the conflict in 2014 or 2015, as evidenced by the crude 'Novorossiya' spray-painted down the side. Later, more systematic and neater methods of denoting unit affiliation were implemented. (Artwork by David Bocquelet)

An example of an MT-LB armoured personnel carrier and artillery tractor, with a modification: a crude, improvised circular turret mounting a 2B9 Vasilek 82mm gun-mortar on the rear deck. The vehicle is marked with 'Republican Guard' and a number 15 in a diamond, the latter an earlier form of tactical marking for DPR vehicles before standardisation, around 2016, on triangles, circles and squares. (Artwork by David Bocquelet)

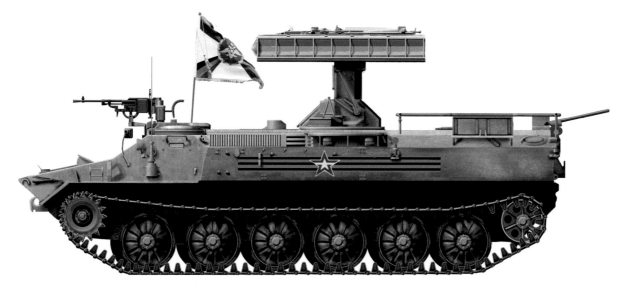

A 9K35 Strela-10 anti-aircraft system (ASCC/NATO-codename 'SA-13 Gopher'), depicted in dark green paint for the 9 May 2021 parade, and carrying the DPR battle flag. The highly mobile Strela-10 was the most capable air defence system openly paraded by the DPR. (Artwork by David Bocquelet)

A BRDM-2 armoured reconnaissance vehicle, captured by the DPR and used in Mariupol in 2014. The application of a crude green and black camouflage scheme was probably as much about differentiating from Ukrainian vehicles of the same type than as effective camouflage per se. This particular vehicle was destroyed in June 2014, as Ukrainian forces regained control of the city centre. (Artworks by David Bocquelet)

Among the improvisations made by the DPR, this combination of an immobilised BMD-2 airborne infantry fighting vehicle on the up-armoured rear of a KamAZ-4310 truck was one of the most unusual. The redundant track links from the BMD-2 have been added to the hull sides for additional protection. The DPR captured a number of BMD IFVs in Sloviansk in 2014 but did not seem to make much use of them, and further examples were not among the vehicles supplied from Russia. This vehicle saw use with Vostok Regiment in the Yasynuvata area from around 2016 onwards. Vostok had a unique black and white camouflage pattern that it applied to certain vehicles, including this one. (Artwork by David Bocquelet)

A BMP-1 infantry fighting vehicle in use by the DPR's armed formations, c. 2016. Extra track links have been added to the turret for additional protection and non-standard thick rubber side skirts and a frontal screen have also been added. The vehicle is painted in the three-tone black/ochre/green camouflage scheme used by contemporaneous Russian Federation forces AFVs. This vehicle, like many DPR armed formation vehicles in the field, bears no unit markings or tactical numbers, making unit attribution difficult. (Artwork by David Bocquelet)

A BMP-2 infantry fighting vehicle, c. early 2016. Thick rubber side skirts have been added, along with metal steps to allow for easier mounting and dismounting. In addition to some light natural camouflage, this vehicle bears a small number '55' in a triangle, associating it with the 5th Separate Motorised Rifle Brigade "Oplot". (Artwork by David Bocquelet)

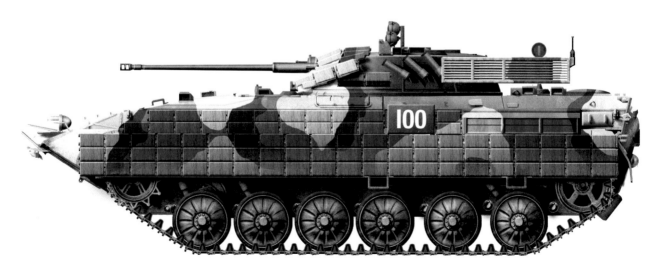

Modified BMP-2 infantry fighting vehicle, 2018. A comprehensive set of Kontakt-1 ERA panels has been added, including around the turret and on the top of the glacis plate. An enlarged turret bustle has also been fitted, giving the turret a modern, diamond-like shape when seen from above. This vehicle, tactical number 100, was painted with a number 53 on the rear doors, suggesting it was in use by the 3rd Separate Motorised Rifle Brigade "Berkut" at the time. (Artwork by David Bocquelet)

A BTR-80 armoured personnel carrier, modified by the DPR with four ATGM launch tubes set around the turret. Though DPR weapons innovation was given less prominence after Zakharchenko's death, it still continued to a lesser degree. This vehicle was exhibited at the 9 May 2020 parade in Donetsk. (Artwork by David Bocquelet)

A 2S1 Gvozdika self-propelled howitzer, c. 2015. During the long and bitterly cold winters in Donbas, DPR vehicles were given winter camouflage schemes, usually comprising of crude whitewash patterns over their usual paint. This Gvozdika wears such a winter colour scheme and flies the flag of Novorossiya. Like many DPR vehicles in the field, it was without any obvious unit or tactical markings. (Artwork by David Bocquelet)

An IS-3 heavy tank, July 2014. This tank was restored and driven off a war memorial plinth in the village of Oleksandro-Kalynove, north of Donetsk, in the early days of the conflict in Donbas. Fitted with a heavy machine gun on the turret, it was painted with anti-Ukrainian slogans, in this case 'To Lvov' (the DPR saw the Ukrainian city of Lviv as being the centre of Ukrainian nationalism). While tactically insignificant, the use of this 1945-era tank had great propaganda value for the DPR. (Artwork by David Bocquelet)

An unusual T-64 variant exhibited by the DPR in the 9 May 2020 parade. Only one example was presented, with a massive amount of Kontakt-1 ERA panelling along the full length of the side skirts, and around a hugely enlarged turret bustle. Little else is known about this variant. The 9 May 2020 parade was also notable for being one in which the vehicles were paraded in three-tone 'field' camouflage, rather than in the parade dark green seen most other years. (Artwork by David Bocquelet)

A parade version of the T-72B main battle tank, put on display for the 9 May parade in 2021, in Donetsk. Painted in dark green overall, the tank is shown flying the ceremonial DPR flag. (Artwork by David Bocquelet)

A T-72B in field use by the DPR, c.2017. Kontakt-1 ERA panels have been knocked loose, and the rear fuel drums are missing. Bright green spray paint has been used to repair the tank's paint in places. (Artwork by David Bocquelet)

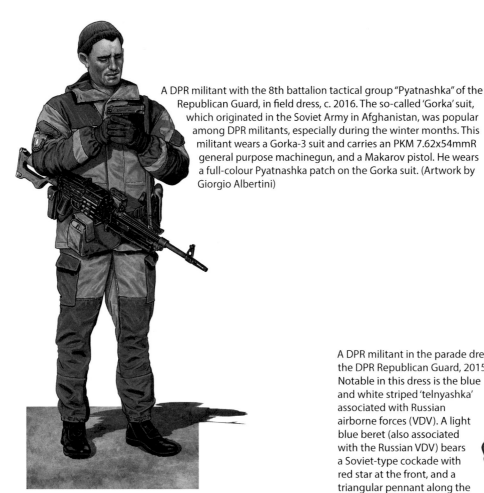

A DPR militant with the 8th battalion tactical group "Pyatnashka" of the Republican Guard, in field dress, c. 2016. The so-called 'Gorka' suit, which originated in the Soviet Army in Afghanistan, was popular among DPR militants, especially during the winter months. This militant wears a Gorka-3 suit and carries an PKM 7.62x54mmR general purpose machinegun, and a Makarov pistol. He wears a full-colour Pyatnashka patch on the Gorka suit. (Artwork by Giorgio Albertini)

A DPR militant in the parade dress of the DPR Republican Guard, 2015. Notable in this dress is the blue and white striped 'telnyashka' associated with Russian airborne forces (VDV). A light blue beret (also associated with the Russian VDV) bears a Soviet-type cockade with red star at the front, and a triangular pennant along the side in the DPR colours. The combat uniform is in three colour digicam, probably a variant of the Russian EMR 'Tetris' design. A white ceremonial belt and full-colour Republican Guard patches are worn. An AK-74M is carried. (Artwork by Giorgio Albertini)

A DPR militant with the 2nd battalion tactical group "Oplot" of the Republican Guard, in field dress, c. 2016. Away from the standardised uniforms visible on parades, DPR militants wore a wide variety of combat uniforms. This militant wears a Soviet-era combat uniform of 'sunray' camouflage pattern. As with many DPR militants in the field, he does not wear name tags or unit patches. (Artwork by Giorgio Albertini)

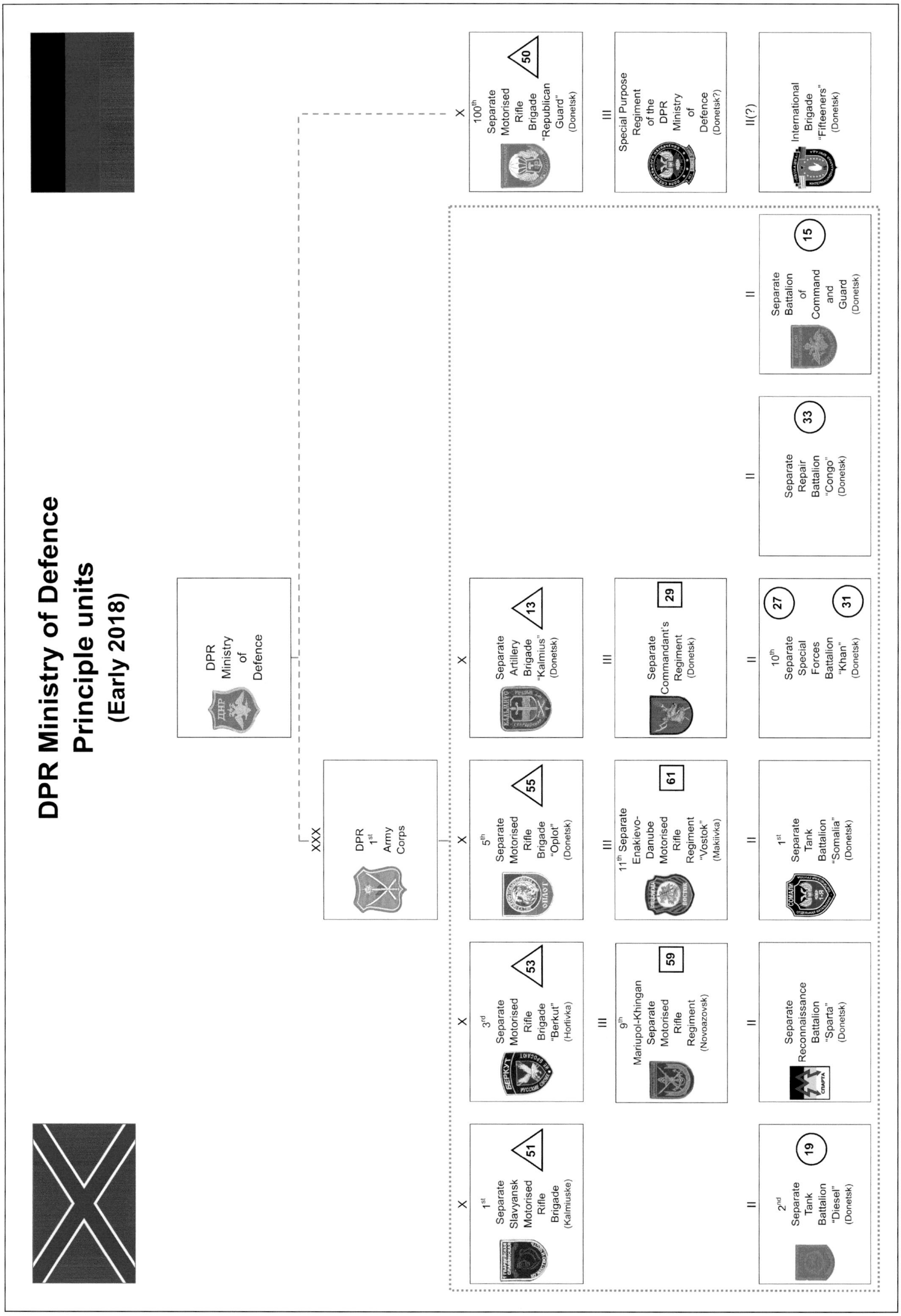

DPR Ministry of Defence
Principle units
(Early 2018)

DPR
Ministry
of
Defence

XXX
DPR
1st
Army
Corps

X
100th
Separate
Motorised
Rifle
Brigade
"Republican
Guard"
(Donetsk)
50

III
Special Purpose
Regiment
of the
DPR
Ministry
of
Defence
(Donetsk?)

II(?)
International
Brigade
"Fifteeners"
(Donetsk)

II
Separate
Battalion
of Command
and
Guard
(Donetsk)
15

II
Separate
Repair
Battalion
"Congo"
(Donetsk)
33

X
Separate
Artillery
Brigade
"Kalmius"
(Donetsk)
13

III
Separate
Commandant's
Regiment
(Donetsk)
29

II
10th
Separate
Special
Forces
Battalion
"Khan"
(Donetsk)
27
31

X
5th
Separate
Motorised
Rifle
Brigade
"Oplot"
(Donetsk)
55

III
11th Separate
Enakievo-
Danube
Motorised
Rifle
Regiment
"Vostok"
(Makiivka)
61

II
1st
Separate
Tank
Battalion
"Somalia"
(Donetsk)

X
3rd
Separate
Motorised
Rifle
Brigade
"Berkut"
(Horlivka)
53

III
9th
Mariupol-Khingan
Separate
Motorised
Rifle
Regiment
(Novoazovsk)
59

II
Separate
Reconnaissance
Battalion
"Sparta"
(Donetsk)

X
1st
Separate
Slavyansk
Motorised
Rifle
Brigade
(Kalmiuske)
51

II
2nd
Separate
Tank
Battalion
"Diesel"
(Donetsk)
19

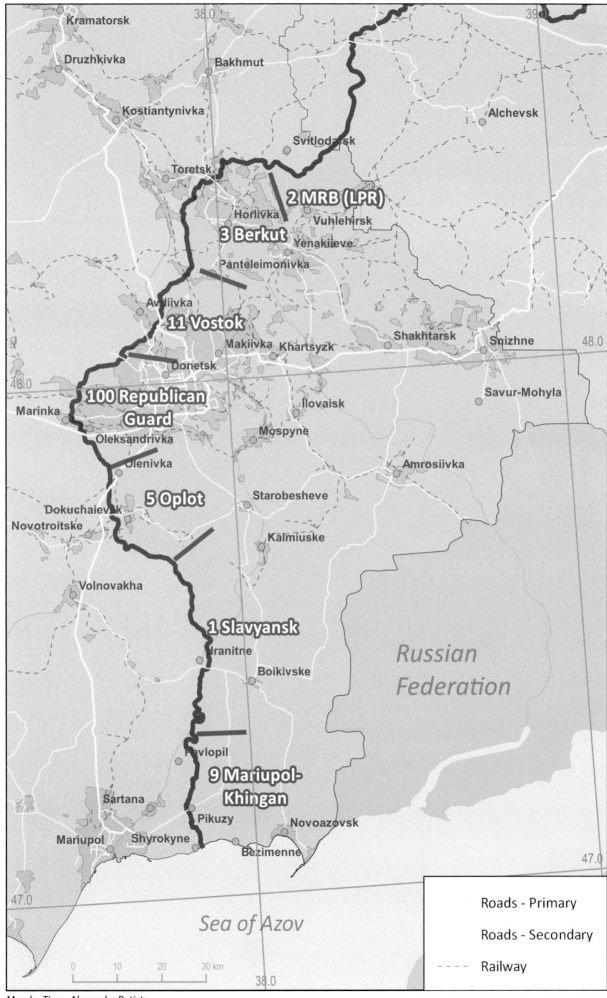

Map by Tiago Alexandre Batista

НЕМОГАЙ
АЛЕКСАНДР СЕРГЕЕВИЧ
09.08.1956 — 08.09.2016

Aleksandr Nemogai, founder and commander of Kalmius. Postcard no. 22 in the set 'Gold Star Heroes', issued by the DPR Ministry of Communication, 2017. (Author's collection)

100th Separate Motorised Rifle Brigade "Republican Guard" (100-я Отдельная Мотострелковая Бригада «Республиканская Гвардия»)

The Republican Guard was created by the decree of the then head of the DPR, Alexander Zakharchenko, on 12 January 2015. Part of its initial strength came from the original Oplot Brigade, which was split in half.25 At its inception, it was not part of the DPR 1st Army Corps, and was directly commanded by Zakharchenko himself.

Republican Guard was set up as a rapid reaction force, with highly mobile units able to be deployed where necessary along the contact line. Internally, Republican Guard was thought to have been organised into at least four battalion tactical groups.

Republican Guard's identity borrowed heavily from the Soviet-era VDV (*Vozdushno-desantnye voyska*, or airborne forces), and Republican Guard soldiers regularly wore light-blue berets and the striped undershirts (тельняшки) associated with VDV forces.

Despite the association with VDV-style uniform, however, the Republican Guard never underwent any specific training associated with airborne forces such as parachute drops, given the total lack of any functioning crewed air assets in the possession of the DPR. Thus, as some observers noted, the self-styled VDV appearance of Republican Guard was more likely part of nation-building via a symbolical association with elite forces.[26] This was reinforced in a 2015 television interview with the then commander of the Republican Guard, in which he noted that the DPR now had 'elite troops' in the manner of other countries.[27]

Overall, the brigade defended a strategically important section of contact line from Olenivka in the south, running around the western side of Donetsk city to Donetsk Airport in the north. Estimates of total strength for the Republican Guard ranged from 3,000 to 5,000 personnel.

Republican Guard reportedly also included units such as 'Patriot,' a special reconnaissance battalion based in the frontline village of Oleksandrivka just southwest of Donetsk, as well as the 'Pyatnashka' battalion, which was strongly associated with volunteer fighters from Abkhazia,[28] another unrecognised state on the territory of Georgia, also supported by the Russian Federation.

Called an 'International Brigade' but operating as something more akin to a battalion, Pyatnashka (literally, 'The Fifteeners') took its name from the 15 original volunteers who arrived in the Donbas at the beginning of the conflict.[29]

Pyatnashka's commander was Akhrik Avidzba, born in Sochi in the Soviet Union in 1986. He participated in the conflict in Abkhazia, and when the fighting in Donbas began, travelled to Donetsk with the first 15 volunteers. The Pyatnashka unit defended an important checkpoint on Stratonahtiv Street in Donetsk, just south of the Donetsk Airport, during the heavy fighting there in 2014.

Its unit patch displays 15 stars for the original volunteers,

Stratonavtiv Street, an important position defended by the Pyatnashka division. (Photograph by Dean O'Brien)

including a black star for one of the members of the unit, Irakli Adleiba, who was killed in June 2015.[30] The patch also includes the flags of the DPR and of Abkhazia. Avidzba was awarded the Hero of the DPR medal.

After Zakharchenko's death in August 2018, and the abolition of the DPR Ministry of Defence, Republican Guard was directly absorbed as a standard brigade into the DPR 1st Army Corps. Its former commander, Ivan Kondratov, was arrested by the DPR in September 2018, part of a purge of commanders who had been loyal to Zakharchenko.

Separate Artillery Brigade "Kalmius" (Отдельная Артиллерийская бригада «Кальмиус»)

Kalmius, which takes its name from one of the main rivers in Donbas, was initially formed of around 500 miners and metallurgical workers, who stormed a Ukrainian military base in Donetsk in June 2014. Acting as one of the DPR's first militia units, later in 2014 it took part in the battles around the memorial hill of Savur-Mohyla and the nearby city of Snizhne.

In October 2014, the unit was reorganised as a separate artillery brigade, and re-equipment began accordingly. The unit was deployed to the cities of Snizhne and Shakhtarsk.

Kalmius Brigade's founder and commander till 2016 was Alexandr Nemogai. Born in 1956, at a young age his family moved to Makiivka in Donetsk oblast. On 8 May 2016 he was awarded the Hero of the DPR medal, but exactly four months later died in unclear circumstances reported to be a targeted assassination, possibly by poisoning.

Notable among Kalmius's officers was Eduard Basurin, who after serving in the brigade became Deputy Defence Minister of the DPR, a post he held until the abolition of the post of Defence Minister in late 2018, following Zakharchenko's death. He was also the main defence spokesperson for the DPR.

The internal structure of the unit is unclear, as like Berkut it maintained a relatively lower profile on social media and other open sources than comparable DPR brigades. The brigade was equipped

Kalmius insignia. Full colour patch, c. 2016. (Author's collection)

with a wide range of equipment including D-30 122mm and Msta-B 152mm towed howitzers, as well as 2S1 Gvozdika, 2S3 Akatsia, 2S5 Giatsint-S and 2S19 Msta-S self-propelled howitzers. MLRS include a number of BM-21 Grad and at least one captured BM-27 Uragan.

In terms of organisation, there were thought to be at least two batteries comprising 2S1 Gvozdika and one battery of BM-21 Grad, but further details of the brigade's internal structure are uncertain.

Mariupol-Khingan insignia. Subdued patch, c. 2018. (Author's collection)

Early pattern full colour Vostok Battalion patch, c. 2014. (Author's collection)

A 2S1 Gvozdika 122mm self-propelled howitzer, parading through Donetsk under the battle flag of the Separate Artillery Brigade "Kalmius" on 9 May 2018. (Private photo collection, used with permission)

9th Mariupol-Khingan Separate Motorised Rifle Regiment (9-й Мариупольско-Хинганский Отдельный Мотострелковый Полк)

The 9th Mariupol-Khingan was formed from the remnants of the Semenovsky Battalion, a loose formation of locals and Russian volunteers who took part in the fighting in Sloviansk and at Donetsk Airport. A reformed and strengthened Semenovsky Battalion then took part in the offensive towards Mariupol, and helped to capture the coastal town of Novoasovsk on 28 August 2014.[31] Later it took part in the bitter fighting for the coastal town of Shyrokyne by the Azov Sea.

The name of the regiment is a pointed nod to a Second World War-era Soviet formation, the 221st Infantry Mariupol-Khingan Red Banner Order of Suvorov Division, which took part in the liberation of Mariupol in October 1943.

In February 2016, the former battalion was reformed into a marine regiment. Amphibious BTR-80 and BTR-70 armoured personnel carriers were supplied, and an unknown mix of T-64BV and T-72B tanks. In terms of artillery, as well as 2S1 self-propelled and D-30 towed howitzers, open-source research suggests the unit was at some point equipped with the 2B16 Nona-K towed mortar,[32] this last system unusual in the conflict in Donbas. Estimated strength in 2018 was around 1,500 people.

The 9th Mariupol-Khingan also utilised around 20 to 25 high speed small boats, which were the DPR's only military maritime assets.[33] These boats were organised into a separate unit, called 'Typhoon.' The boats, rigid hulled fishing craft, crewed by two or three DPR militants in each vessel, were armed with heavy machine guns and AGS-17 automatic grenade launchers.[34]

The unit was headquartered in the coastal town of Novoazovsk, and deployed in the towns and positions along the southern section of the contact line from just east of Shyrokyne and northwards, including the heavily fought-over frontline village of Pikuzy (formerly Kominternove)[35]. Given its geographical location, the 9th Mariupol-Khingan had to closely cooperate with units from the 1st Slavyansk which was deployed on the 9th Mariupol-Khingan's northern flank.

11th Separate Enakievo-Danube Motorised Rifle Regiment "Vostok" (11 отдельный Енакиевско-Дунайский мотострелковый полк «Восток»)

The Vostok Regiment was one of the most well-known of the DPR armed formations outside Ukraine, probably owing to the level of publicity that surrounded it in the early stages of the conflict, and the heated dispute over its origins. It also swiftly established a reputation for being one of the most disciplined and combat effective DPR units.[36]

On 4 May 2014, a small group of volunteers, including former employees of the Ukrainian State Security Service (SBU), as well as volunteers from Ossetia and Chechenya, seized an SBU office in Donetsk.[37] It was a former member of the Ukrainian SBU's Alpha Group, Alexander Khodakovsky, who later became the commander of the Vostok Regiment.

The Vostok Battalion (as it was initially) was officially founded two days later. Despite reorganisations, which will be discussed

A position of the Vostok regiment, one of the best known DPR formations, in Yasynuvata. (Photograph by Dean O'Brien)

Initial reports in some Western-oriented media outlets suggested that the unit was a resurrection of a unit created by the Russian GRU during the conflict in South Ossetia,[38] a rumour which persisted. However more nuanced analysis suggests that this is unlikely to be the case and that – while acknowledging the presence of volunteers from the Caucasus region in the unit[39] – suggests that there are no historical links to a unit disbanded at the end of the Georgian conflict in 2008.[40]

In the initial stages of the fighting, the Vostok Regiment took part in capturing the small town of Panteleimonivka, helping to create a link for DPR forces between the major cities of Donetsk and Horlivka. Later, it took part in the fierce fighting for Donetsk Airport in late 2014.

below, the unit was still widely referred to in Ukrainian, Russian and DPR media as the 'Vostok Battalion.'

Like many of the major DPR armed formations, the unit saw a lot of reorganisation after its inception. Towards the end of 2014

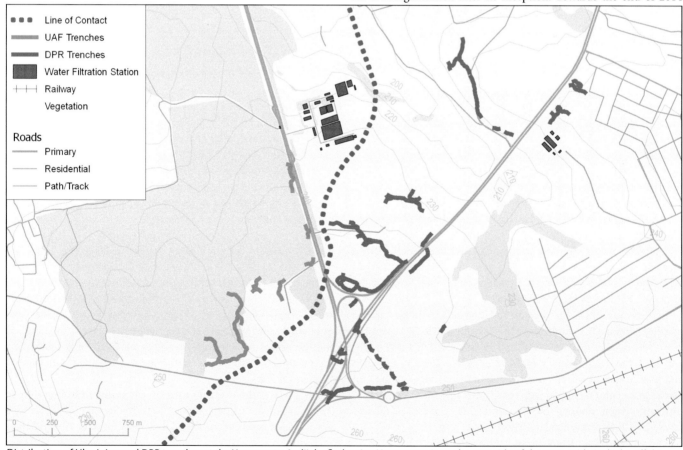

Distribution of Ukrainian and DPR trenches at the Yasynuvata-Avdiivka flashpoint. Yasynuvata is on the east side of the map, with Avdiivka off the map to the northwest. At the major road junction where the H20 (left) and M04 (right) highways met, Ukrainian and DPR frontline trenches were less than 200m apart. The critically important Donetsk Water Filtration Station found itself in a dangerous location effectively between the two sides. DPR units at this location were from Vostok Regiment. Contour heights are in metres. Map based on openly available commercial satellite imagery dated 2019. (Map by Tiago Alexandre Batista)

Mid pattern full colour Vostok patch, with the unit listed as a 'Special Brigade' (Спецбригада), c. 2015. (Author's collection)

Enakievo-Danube Motorised Rifle Regiment insignia. Late pattern subdued patch, c. 2016. (Author's collection)

the then Vostok Battalion was first upgraded to a 'Special Battalion' (Спецбригада), and then in 2015 changed again to the 11th Separate Enakievo-Danube Motorised Rifle Regiment "Vostok" within DPR 1st Army Corps.[41]

There is some evidence to suggest that the subordination of Vostok into the DPR 1st Army Corp was resisted by many of its personnel, who saw it as a means of restricting Khodakovsky's personal influence within the DPR.[42] Khodakovsky later attempted to set up a political party, which was refused participation in the 2018 DPR elections.

The Vostok Regiment was deployed to the important railway junction city of Yasynuvata to the northeast of Donetsk, at the Yasynuvata-Avdiivka flashpoint, as well as to further locations between Donetsk and Horlivka including Spartak.

A BMP-1 infantry fighting vehicle bearing the flag of the 11th Separate Enakievo-Danube Motorised Rifle Regiment "Vostok", parading through Donetsk on 9 May 2019. (Private photo collection, used with permission)

Vostok used a wide range of armoured vehicles, including tanks, armoured personnel carriers like the BTR-80, and a mixture of other vehicles, including some improvised armoured vehicles. One notable example, often rolled out for the unit's numerous online videos, was the body of an immobilised BMD-2 infantry fighting vehicle, mounted in the back of an up-armoured KamAZ 4310 truck, creating an improvised 'gun truck' painted in Vostok's distinctive and unique black and white camouflage pattern.

In addition to these improvised vehicles, in late 2014 Vostok displayed a captured Ukrainian BTR-4 infantry fighting vehicle, armed with a 30mm cannon. The captured vehicle, painted in a dark green, had the Vostok insignia on the turret and hull. Some initial suggestions that the photo had been photoshopped were disproved by a lengthy YouTube video in which Vostok militants were seen test-driving it.[43]

The unit also undertook modifications to improve the armour of their BMP infantry fighting vehicles. The tank battalion in Vostok was considered to be dangerous and combat effective by Ukrainian forces, and extensive modification of the unit's tanks was often observed, setting them apart in this respect from other DPR armed formations. Modifications included improvised side skirts, or extra panels of Kontakt-1 ERA.

The total strength of Vostok was estimated between 2,000 and 4,000 personnel. In a social media post in mid-2017 reported on Ukrainian media, Khodakovsky reported that 500 members of the Vostok Regiment had been killed, out of a total of 4,000.[44]

For a time, it counted within its ranks sub-units such as 'Essence of Time', which later went to the 10th Separate Special Operations Battalion 'Khan', and the 'Miners' Division', part of which was later absorbed into the Kalmius Brigade.[45] Other sub-units included a number of companies named after the places where they drew the majority of the members, including Khartsyzk Company and Makeyevka[46] Company.

Special Purpose Regiment of the DPR Ministry of Defence (Полк специального назначения Министерства обороны ДНР)

The unit was formed in April 2016. Also known as the Regiment of Special Forces of the Head of the DPR, like Republican Guard, it was another unit formed directly under the command of Aleksander Zakharchenko. After his death in 2018, the unit was disbanded and the component battalions reportedly transferred to the Internal Troops of the DPR Ministry of Internal Affairs.

The regiment was commanded by a Yevgeny Ryadnov, a resident of Kostiantynivka who participated in the capture of Vuhlehirsk. In an interesting vignette into the motivation of senior DPR militants, in a 2018 interview he described his motivations for joining the

Full colour Special Purpose Regiment of the DPR Ministry of Defence patch, c. 2018. The four stars represented the four component battalions within the Regiment. (Author's collection)

DPR armed formations, which included the 'betrayal' of the Soviet Army in Germany after the fall of the Berlin Wall, and what he saw as the subsequent encroachment of NATO into Ukraine.[47]

It initially comprised three battalions: Chechen, Pyatnashka, and Patriot, later joined by a fourth, Prilepin. Pyatnashka and Patriot were both battalions from Republican Guard, it is unclear if they were fully transferred to the Special Purpose Regiment (while it existed) or if they were somehow subdivided.

The unit's insignia had four stars to symbolise these four battalions.[48] Elements of Chechen, including at least one BTR-

'Work, brothers!' A commemoration of the commander of Sparta Battalion, with his call sign 'Motorola' written on the St. George's ribbon. Magnet, c. 2018. (Author's collection)

ПАВЛОВ
АРСЕН СЕРГЕЕВИЧ

02.02.1983 — 16.10.2016

Arsen Pavlov, commander of Sparta Battalion. Postcard no. 8 in the set 'Gold Star Heroes', issued by the DPR Ministry of Communication, 2017. (Author's collection)

МОТОРОЛА
ПАВЛОВ
Арсен Сергеевич
02.02.1983 - 16.10.2016

The grave of Arsen Pavlov, also known as Motorola, at Donetsk Sea Cemetery. (Photograph by Dean O'Brien)

80 armoured personnel carrier, were sent by Zakharchenko into Luhansk in 2017 in support of the 'coup' that removed LPR leader Igor Plotnitsky.[49]

Prilepin Battalion was founded by the Russian writer Zakhar Prilepin. He had been an advisor to Zakharchenko in 2015, and after the deaths of the DPR commanders Givi and Motorola decided to form his own battalion. Prilepin Battalion was formed in October 2016 and was based in the Hotel Prague in central Donetsk.[50] When the Special Purpose Regiment was disbanded in late 2018, it was reported that Prilepin Battalion resisted the move, and a firefight resulted at the Hotel Prague.[51]

Separate Reconnaissance Battalion "Sparta" (Отдельный разведывательный батальон «Спарта»)

Sparta Battalion exhibited many of the traits of the DPR units that survived the reorganisation and consolidation of DPR armed formations: wide recognition, a charismatic leader, and an unusual and seemingly entirely organic unit symbology that defies easy characterisation. Formed in the initial stages of the fighting in Slavyansk, the unit was for the first two years commanded by Arsen Pavlov, who arrived in Donbas in 2014 with the 'Crimea Company' group of fighters led by Igor Girkin.[52]

Pavlov, a Russian citizen who went by the nom de guerre 'Motorola' owing to his background in a signals unit in the Russian

Sparta Battalion patch. Full colour, c. 2016. (Author's collection)

Sparta Battalion militants riding a BTR-80 armoured personnel carrier at the 9 May parade. The AK-74M rifles and underslung GP-25 grenade launchers have been painted with a Soviet 'sun ray' camouflage pattern. Donetsk, 2019. (Private photo collection, used with permission)

sides of the contact line, and probably was a factor in its retention as a distinct unit.

Somalia was formed from small units that fought in the battles around Ilovaisk in 2014, and was commanded in its first few years by Mikhail Tolstykh, a native of Ilovaisk who went by the nom de guerre 'Givi.' Like Pavlov, the former leader of Sparta Battalion, Tolstykh attained an almost cult status in the DPR media, originating from a famous TV interview in which he retained his composure as 122mm Grad rockets exploded close by.[59]

The name of the unit supposedly derived from the 'irregular' look of its first fighters, and got its name because when fighters lined up for the first time '…they were dressed in all manner of civilian clothes, such as shorts and trainers, did not look like a combat force, and, in their view, resembled Somali pirates.'[60]

Tolstykh was killed in an explosion at his Donetsk apartment in February 2017, the weapon used was reportedly an RPO-A Shmel thermobaric rocket launcher. Again, this attack was blamed on Ukrainian special forces or 'foreign' sabotage groups by the DPR authorities, but was more likely some form of internal action related to the removal of DPR unit commanders. Both Pavlov (of Sparta Battalion) and Tolstykh appeared on the first DPR stamp issued in May 2015.

Though called a tank battalion, it was also varyingly referred to as a 'Separate Battalion Tactical Group' or 'Separate Assault Battalion.' Somalia took part in the battles for Donetsk Airport. Based in Donetsk, in the vicinity of the airport, the unit reportedly possessed

Army, quickly became very prominent in the media on both sides of the line of contact. His much-publicised wedding in Donetsk, attended by Igor Girkin, became such a symbol of the DPR that it was repeatedly presented in highly unflattering fictionalised forms in the Ukrainian media, such as in the 2018 film *Donbass*.[53]

Sparta Battalion was involved in some of the key battles in eastern Ukraine, including that for Donetsk Airport and at Ilovaisk and Debaltseve. The unit had a highly controversial reputation, with numerous credible allegations of involvement in war crimes.[54]

In October 2016 Pavlov was killed by the explosion of a bomb in the lift of his Donetsk apartment building.[55] Though the death was swiftly blamed by the DPR on Ukrainian special forces operating within Donetsk, it is far more likely he was removed as part of a wider attempt to silence the more controversial and extreme DPR unit commanders. In the DPR and Russian Federation, Motorola was posthumously lionised, and a documentary film devoted to his exploits called *His Battalion* premiered in St Petersburg in 2017.[56]

The unit probably numbered around several hundred core members, organised into at least three companies, and was sometimes referred to as belonging to the Marine Corps. This was apparently owing to Pavlov, who introduced many symbolic attributes of a Soviet Marine Corps unit.[57]

Sparta regularly took part in the annual Donetsk 9 May Victory Day parades, with its militants sitting on top of BTR-80 armoured personnel carriers. The unit had an unusual symbology, with its insignia a mix of the black/white/yellow Imperial Russian flag, atop which was a stylised lightning bolt 'M' apparently taken from the '2033' series of science-fiction books and video games.[58] This pastiche of new and old was common across DPR propaganda and symbology.

1st Separate Tank Battalion "Somalia" (1-й Отдельный танковый батальон «Сомали»)

Along with Sparta, the Somalia Battalion was a unit which 'survived' through the reorganisation of DPR units. In a similar manner to Sparta, its unique character became familiar in the media on both

Somalia Battalion insignia. Here the unit is described as a 'Separate Assault Battalion'. Full colour patch, c. 2016. (Author's collection)

A depiction of Mikhail Tolstykh, commander of Somalia Battalion. Such was his recognition in the DPR that no explanatory name or text was evidently felt necessary. Magnet, c. 2018. (Author's collection)

Mikhail Tolstykh, commander of Somalia Battalion until his death in 2017. Postcard no. 10 in the set 'Gold Star Heroes', issued by the DPR Ministry of Communication, 2017. (Author's collection)

a company of T-64 tanks, as well as three motorised rifle companies equipped with BMP infantry fighting vehicles, an unknown number of artillery pieces, and the usual complement of anti-tank weapons and small arms.

2nd Separate Tank Battalion "Diesel" (2-й Отдельный танковый батальон «Дизель»)

Diesel was the best known DPR tank unit and had a much clearer identity as a tank unit than Sparta. Diesel was thought to comprise four companies of 10 tanks each, as well as a motorised rifle company equipped with 10 BMP infantry fighting vehicles.[61]

Equipped with T-72 series main battle tanks, the main vehicle seen in open-source media in service with Diesel was the T-72B[62], though there is some evidence to suggest that some T-72B Model 1989 main battle tanks were also supplied to the unit, cascaded down from Russian Federation armoured brigades which had been re-equipped with more advanced T-72B3 main battle tanks in 2015.[63] Tanks in Diesel were generally painted in the modern three-tone camouflage scheme also seen in the Russian Federation armed forces, comprising green, yellow-ochre and black.

Headquartered in Donetsk, Diesel also had a significant presence around the large DPR tank training range southeast of the town of Ternove, some 60km east of Donetsk. While daytime sightings of DPR tanks became rare in the area close to the contact line – as tanks were forbidden within 15km of the contact line under the Minsk Agreements – in the rear areas of the DPR vast weapons cantonment and training areas were built up, in particular at Ternove.

Easily visible on commercial satellite imagery, at Ternove huge rectangular cantonment yards were constructed, surrounded by fencing and trenches, and capable of housing several hundred armoured fighting vehicles at a time. Around these cantonment areas was a huge training area including tank firing ranges.

On these training ranges, Diesel participated in tank 'biathlons' which pitted Diesel against other tank units from the DPR and LPR. One video about a biathlon in 2017 included an interview with a female T-72 tank commander in Diesel, an example of female participation across the DPR's armed formations, including in combat roles.[64]

Diesel was commanded for many years by a Pyotr Ruchyev, who was reportedly detained in the DPR in late 2021, accused of 'financial crimes.'[65] This is probably another example of the fractious

The grave of Mikhail Tolstykh ('Givi') at Donetsk Sea Cemetery. (Photograph by Dean O'Brien)

Diesel Separate Tank Battalion insignia. Subdued patch, c. 2018. (Author's collection)

nature of the DPR, in particular with unit commanders who were seen as becoming too 'autonomous.'

10th Separate Special Operations Battalion "Khan" (10-й Отдельный батальон специального назначения «Хан»)

'Khan' was the highest profile special operations unit in the DPR. Formed in December 2014, it conducted reconnaissance and combat missions along the line of contact. Nominated a special operations unit, Khan was evidently a well-equipped unit, even by 2015 it had already been equipped with modern Russian-pattern helmets, body armour and small arms. Vehicles included heavily up-armoured versions of the Ural-4320,[66] and BMP-2 infantry fighting vehicles.

One major sub-unit was the 1st Special Operations Company 'Essence of Time' (Суть времени), which had previously been in Vostok Regiment and was moved to Khan in June 2015. 'Essence of Time' comprised a small unit of members dispatched to the DPR from the Russian political movement of the same name. Truly neo-Soviet in nature, one of the movement's principal goals was the reinstatement of the Soviet Union. Some of the members of early iterations of the company had met at Essence of Time's political schools in Russia, years before the start of the conflict.

In practical terms, 'Essence of Time' Company was able to rely on the political movement in Russia for equipment, including radios, PPE, helmets, rangefinders and medical kit.[67] In keeping with the political and propaganda aims of its parent movement in Russia, the 'Essence of Time' Company engaged in an intense information warfare campaign, publishing numerous videos of its combat activities.

Other 1st Army Corps Units

Beyond the main units listed above, were numerous other, smaller DPR armed formation units about which much less is known. One of the only other 'named' units within 1st Army Corps not listed above was a Separate Repair Battalion "Kongo." There was also a Battalion of Command and Guard (Батальон Управления и Охраны).

The DPR's Separate Commandant's Regiment (Отдельный Комендантский Полк) operated under the DPR Ministry of Defence, with unit number 08816. Its logo comprised a dog's head with crossed broom and halberd, set on a red background.[68] The regiment included military police units, who wore large black brassards bearing the dog's head patch below the DPR flag.

In 2015 the DPR created a Higher Combined Arms Command School (Донецкого Высшего Общевойскового Командного Училища, abbreviated in Russian to ДонВОКУ or DonVOKU in English). This became the principle school for training officers for the DPR's armed formations, and was located on the former territory of the Soviet-era Military and Political School for Engineering and Signal Troops in Donetsk.[69] DonVOKU was headed by a Major General Tikhonov, who had previously commanded Oplot. A Zakharchenko-era creation, it survived the dissolution of the DPR Ministry of Defence and continued its activities into 2019 and beyond.

One DPR unit about which little is known is the 384th Separate Naval Special Reconnaissance unit (384-й Отдельный морской разведывательный пункт специального назначения, 384-й ОМРП СпН). A relative latecomer to the DPR 1st Army Corps order of battle, it was formed in August 2021.[70] Like the 9th Mariupol-Khingan, it was named after a Second World War-era unit, in this case the 384th Marine Battalion of the Soviet Black Sea Fleet. Deployed in Bezimenne, it was reported to include among its members a number of ethnic Greeks[71] from the DPR and LPR. Its internal organisation included three companies of special purpose. In March 2022, it was involved in the combined DPR/Russian Federation assault on Mariupol. Little else on this unit was openly available at the time of writing.

Higher Combined Arms Command School insignia. Subdued patch, c. 2018. (Author's collection)

Battalion of Command and Guard, Armed Forces of the DPR insignia. Subdued patch, c. 2018. (Author's collection)

8

ARMED FORMATIONS OF THE DPR NOT FALLING UNDER 1ST ARMY CORPS

As a heavily militarised society, the DPR created a number of other armed formations that did not come under the control of the DPR 1st Army Corps. Only units of a military or paramilitary nature are discussed, for reasons of scope the units of the DPR police, among which light weapons were widespread, will not be discussed. This also applies to the MGB, i.e. the DPR Ministry of State Security (ДНР Министерство Государственной Безопасности), which conducted internal security and border guard tasks, and which was modelled on the KGB.

The presence of heavily armed units affiliated with nominally 'civilian' DPR ministries reportedly caused ill-feeling among some of the DPR 1st Army Corps commanders. Khodakovsky complained that "Vityaz", which was controlled by the DPR Ministry of Transport, had seventeen 12.7mm NSV heavy machineguns, more than the entire Vostok Regiment at the time.[1] After the death of Zakharchenko, most of these units were incorporated into either DPR 1st Army Corps or the Internal Troops of the Ministry of Internal Affairs.

This section will aim to provide an overview of some of the most significant of these units – it is not intended as a comprehensive list.

Internal Troops of the Ministry of Internal Affairs of the DPR

The creation of the Internal Troops of the Ministry of Internal Affairs (Внутренние войска Министерства внутренних дел ДНР) were formed in March 2015, with their tasks and functions based on their Russian Federation equivalent.[2] These were thought to include at least two regiments of Internal Troops, as well as a special regiment of police troops called "Bastion" which was headquartered in Donetsk. In the reorganisation of the DPR's armed formations, some

part of Vostok Regiment also went to the Internal Troops, and came to be based on the south side of Yasynuvata.

In practice, differences in equipment were observed, with Internal Troops generally using older equipment than 1st Army Corps units. For example, Internal Troops utilised older versions of the Ural truck, such as the 375D, compared to 1st Army Corps units which by 2018 had been equipped with late-model Ural 4320 or 43206s.

Special Risk Detachment "Legion" of the Ministry of Emergency Situations of the DPR (Отряд по проведению специальных спасательных работ особого риска «Легион» МЧС ДНР)

Modelled on its equivalent in the Russian Federation, the DPR Ministry of Emergency Situations (MChS) was a paramilitary civil-defence organisation, which also had charge of the fire service, explosive ordnance disposal, and other rescue-type work. In the DPR, the MChS also operated its own military unit, "Legion." The unit reportedly took part in the battles at Donetsk Airport, Ilovaisk and Debaltseve, among others.

Legion reportedly never comprised more than around 500 personnel, and operated a small number of armoured vehicles including a reported three T-64 tanks, and BMP-1 and BMP-2 infantry fighting vehicles. It was commanded in 2018 by a Colonel Sergey Zavdoveev.

In a 2018 video, what was probably a significant proportion (if not all) of Legion's armoured vehicles at the time was demonstrated.[3] In the video were two operational T-64s (with a further one out of commission in the background), two BMP-1 and one BMP-2 infantry fighting vehicles, one BMD-2 infantry fighting vehicle with upgraded PL-1-01 spotlight mounted, and one BTR-80 armoured

'Dear employees of the DPR MGB! I congratulate you on the 100th anniversary of the foundation of the organs of state security. Head of the DPR A. V. Zakharchenko.' Like much DPR propaganda messaging, this poster draws an implied historical link from the DPR MGB of 2017 back to the founding of the Soviet NKVD in 1917. Donetsk, December 2017. (Private photo collection, used with permission)

Special Risk Detachment "Legion" insignia. Subdued patch, c. 2016. (Author's collection)

personnel carrier with TKN-4GA-01 commander's sight and improvised armour sheets on the upper hull sides. The vehicles bore a rather crude green, black and white 'winter' camouflage pattern, and all had the unit number '88' in a white rhombus on their turrets.

Legion was incorporated into the Internal Troops of the Ministry of Internal Affairs towards the end of 2018.

Republican State Security Organisation RGSO (Республиканской Государственной Службы Охраны РГСО)

The RGSO was founded on 22 February 2016, and performed a number of functions including providing a bodyguard unit to the head of the DPR, Aleksandr Zakharchenko. From 2016 to 2018 it was an influential unit, with powers to access any DPR office or property at will. Its roles and responsibilities overlapped with that of the DPR MGB.

RGSO took part in the 2017 'coup' in the LPR, during which Zakharchenko sent RGSO units to support the removal of Igor Plotnitsky. Shortly after Zakharchenko's death, the RGSO was disbanded in late 2018, with its units transferred to either the 1st Army Corps or the Ministry of Internal Affairs.[4]

Other units

Other DPR armed formation units about which relatively little is known include the Special forces of the DPR Ministry of Taxes and Duties (Спецназ министерства налогов и сборов), and the Special purpose unit of the Ministry of Transport of the DPR "Vityaz" (Подразделение спецназначения "Витязь" Министерства транспорта ДНР).

Vityaz was formally tasked with protection of railway infrastructure, and was presented with an official battle standard in February 2016.[5] However, both may have been partly utilised – in the same way as RGSO – as bodyguard units for the senior DPR ministers in charge of the respective ministries. Both units were disbanded at the end of 2018.

RGSO commemorative stamp and first day envelope. On the stamp, Zakharchenko is pictured flanked by four RGSO members. The building in the background was the Donetsk Regional State Administration building. Stamp and envelope issued 18 September 2017. (Author's collection)

9
WEAPONRY AND EQUIP-MENT

by the DPR it could be said that it was artificially 'frozen' in the late Soviet-era equipment of the 1980s and early 1990s.

This section will discuss the weaponry and equipment in use by the DPR's armed formations, based on open-source research. As with other aspects of the conflict in eastern Ukraine, it is difficult at times using only open sources to differentiate between the regular forces of the Russian Federation – deployed in strength in the period between late 2014 and early 2015 – and those of the DPR's armed formations. This

The military equipment utilised by the armed forces of the DPR became a subject of great interest to Ukrainian and Western observers. This intense scrutiny usually had two main and interlocking objectives, to hunt for so-called 'flag' items which would prove supply by external powers (in particular the Russian Federation), and to prove that items used by the DPR could not have originated in pre-conflict stockpiles.

At a session at the International Court of Justice in the Hague in 2017, in a case between Ukraine and the Russian Federation over the conflict in Ukraine, one of the representatives from the Russian Federation suggested that the main source of weapons for the armed forces of both the DPR and LPR were '…stockpiles inherited by Ukraine in 1991 from the Soviet Army that was formerly tasked to hold off the entire NATO. A lot of these stockpiles were deposited in the old mines of Donbass and later captured by rebels. Another source of weapons was the retreating Ukrainian army itself.'[1]

These claims were roundly discredited by numerous detailed pieces of investigative journalism by organisations such as Bellingcat, and the resulting rounds of claim and counter-claim were very much part of the ongoing information warfare that accompanied the conflict in eastern Ukraine between 2014 and early 2022.

In the initial stages of the fighting in eastern Ukraine, the then nascent forces of the DPR utilised a wide variety of weapons, in what one 2014 research report referred to as a 'rag-tag assemblage of older and expedient types … in use with pro-Russian militants in eastern Ukraine.'[2] As the conflict has gone on, however, the armed formations of the DPR underwent a certain standardisation of weaponry of all classes.

In terms of weaponry – but particularly armoured vehicles and artillery – the supply to the DPR was of a particular type, which was evidently carefully designed by the Kremlin to mirror the types of vehicles that could plausibly have been found in stockpiles or captured from Ukrainian forces in the early stages of the conflict. Therefore, in terms of the majority of the military equipment used

is equally true of weapons and equipment.

Broadly speaking, though small arms, armoured vehicles and artillery were clearly widely employed by the DPR's armed formations, wide question marks remain over the DPR's independent capabilities in terms of UAVs, electronic warfare and to a certain extent advanced air defence systems. This blurring between regular Russian forces deployed in Donbas and the DPR's armed formations was a feature of the Kremlin's actual and information war. As this volume focuses on the DPR's armed formations, it will attempt to lay out those weapon systems reliably recorded in the hands of those formations.

Small Arms

In the case of small arms, for example, the wide variety of weapons seen in the early stages of the conflict in mid-2014 – many probably drawn from civilian shooting groups, museums, and military re-enactment groups – have been replaced by a standardised set of weapons based around the 5.45mm AK-74 assault rifle and variants.

Support weapons such as the 5.54x39mm RPK-74 light machine gun and the 7.62x54mmR PKM general purpose machine gun were widespread in the DPR's armed formations. There is also evidence of some examples of the 7.62x54mmR PKP Pecheneg general purpose machine gun in use, with such weapons seen on social media accounts linked to Sparta Battalion[3] and Oplot Brigade and one captured in 2015 by the Ukrainian armed forces near Marinka.[4]

Heavier machineguns included the commonplace 12.7×108mm DShK and 12.7x108mm NSV. Limited numbers of the modern 12.7x108mm 6P50 Kord heavy machinegun have also been identified in DPR armed formation hands, again a 'flag' item that was of interest to Ukrainian open-source researchers.

With the relative solidification of the contact line between mid-2015 and early 2022, the importance of sniper rifles increased, as this form of weaponry caused a high proportion of military and civilian casualties during this period. By 2020, it was estimated that

A Kalmius Brigade DPR militant carries a 5.45mm AK-74M, by far the most widespread assault rifle used by the DPR armed formations. 9 May parade, 2019. (Private photo collection, used with permission)

approximately a third of all Ukrainian military casualties were being caused by sniper fire.[5]

7.62×54mmR SVDM and SVDS sniper rifles, 9mm VSS Vintorez, and 12.7mm ASVK sniper rifles were all reliably documented in use by DPR personnel. At the 2018 Victory Day parade, Sparta Battalion militants included in the parade carried 12.7mm OSV-96 anti-materiel rifles. The bitter sniper war that the DPR armed formations and Ukrainian armed forces fought across the contact line was an area in which female DPR militants were often prominent, with female snipers in operation on both sides.

Anti-Tank and Light Support Weapons

Rocket-propelled grenade launchers were a common weapon, with modern types like the RPG-22 one-shot disposable rocket launcher quickly arriving in Sloviansk along with Girkin's initial 'Crimea Company.'

The venerable RPG-7 rocket-propelled grenade launcher saw widespread use among the DPR's armed formations. Various warheads were used with the RPG-7 launchers, including the 'original' PG-7 HEAT warhead as well as modernised PG-7M and PG-7L HEAT rounds.

The reusable flexibility of the RPG-7, compared to more modern disposable RPG launchers, allowed the DPR armed formations to utilise the weapons system in

various unconventional ways. One method of employment saw the use of the RPG-7 to launch POM-2 anti-personnel mines at Ukrainian positions at the southern end of the line of contact near Shyrokyne and Pikuzy.[6] This allowed POM-2 mines to be dropped onto Ukrainian positions at a reported maximum range of around 500m, where the mines would then activate themselves and detonate either via activation of the mine's tripwires or the timed self-destruct mechanism. Another unusual usage, recorded on social media, was the practice of using the RPG-7 to launch modified 82mm mortar rounds.[7]

The SPG-9 Kopye 73mm recoilless gun was also a common weapon across all DPR units. Firing HE and HEAT rounds, it was commonly emplaced in or near frontline DPR positions.

The 9K113 Konkurs Soviet-era SACLOS wire-guided anti-tank missile was also used by the DPR's armed formations. In the static warfare across the contact line, it saw use as a 'bunker buster' in addition to its anti-armour role.

The MT-12 Rapira 100m Soviet-era towed anti-tank gun was widely distributed, either towed by truck or MT-LB armoured personnel carriers. It served more as a form of light artillery piece,

DPR sniper team, with 7.62×54mmR SVDM, riding on a quadbike at the 2018 9 May parade. (Private photo collection, used with permission)

especially given its effectiveness against main battle tanks would be questionable.

In terms of other infantry support weapons, the AGS-17 Plamya and AGS-30 30mm automatic grenade launchers were a common sight among DPR formations, as well as 82mm and 120mm mortars.

Landmines

Both sides in the conflict in Donbas made extensive use of anti-tank landmines, for the purposes of obstructing or channelling enemy movement. This became especially prevalent as the contact line solidified and both sides dug in to static positions.

Metal bodied TM-62M and plastic TM-62P3 anti-tank mines were a common feature on the battlefields of Donbas, and it has been noted that anti-tank minefields were often surface-laid.

Open-source research has shown that at least some of the mines in use by the armed formations of the DPR and LPR were made after 1991 in factories in Russia.[8] The DPR also deployed the TM-83 off-route directional anti-vehicle mine, which utilises acoustic sensors to identify targets, before hitting them with a shaped charge as they pass the mine's location.

Other mines laid by the DPR included OZM-72 bounding fragmentation mines, MON-50, MON-90 and MON-100 directional fragmentation mines, as well as PMN-2 anti-personnel blast mines. PMN-2 mines are of particular note as Ukraine has reportedly never possessed anti-personnel mines of this type.[9] While the use of PMN-2 anti-personnel mines by the DPR has been widely documented, the reported deployment of the more modern PMN-4 anti-personnel blast mine is much less certain and cannot be reliably confirmed.

Main Battle Tanks

Both symbolically and practically, main battle tanks were at the core of the DPR's armed formations. The introduction of these main battle tanks into the DPR's armed formations marked a major

escalation of the conflict. The first T-64s and T-72s began appearing in the hands of the DPR and LPR in June 2014, most moving across the border from the Russian Federation.

One report on the conflict noted how before 12 June 2014, '... there was no evidence that tanks were being used by the Russian-backed fighters'[10] in Donbas. From June 2014 onwards the situation changed suddenly, as the DPR began fielding T-64s in increasing numbers, far beyond the number of tanks that they could reasonably claim to have captured from the Ukrainian armed forces. In addition to the tanks themselves was a reliable fuel supply chain stretching back into Russia, crossing the border in places where the Ukrainian armed forces were no longer operating. This was equally vital in keeping these thirsty vehicles operating.

Ukrainian sources repeatedly noted that the serial numbers of tanks captured from the armed formations of the DPR did not match those ever on the inventory of the Ukrainian armed forces. Clearly, the T-64s being supplied to the DPR were being drawn from extensive stockpiles in the Russian Federation.

The presence of the T-64 main battle tank in large numbers on both sides of the conflict in Donbas was a unique feature of the conflict in Ukraine. The DPR units mostly had possession of the T-64BV, an upgraded version of the T-64B featuring Kontakt-1 explosive reactive armour on the glacis plate, side skirts and turret. Earlier T-64B variants were also present.

Never exported by the Soviet Union, and assigned to elite tank units facing NATO forces in Western Europe, the T-64 was inherited by the armed forces of both Ukraine and the Russian Federation after the dissolution of the Soviet Union. The T-64 was imbued with particular importance, both practically and symbolically, in Ukraine, as the Kharkiv Morozov Machine-building Design Bureau where the T-64 was designed and built was located in the country. This factory, and associated defence plants across Ukraine, allowed the country to continue to repair and upgrade the T-64 as needed.

Extensive use of landmines necessitated the means to counter them. A T-64B demonstrates its KMT mine rollers on a demonstration run for the DPR media. Environs of Debaltseve, 2017. (Private photo collection, used with permission)

Tank troops of the DPR. Magnet, c. 2016. (Author's collection)

None of these were combat-ready when the fighting erupted in the east of Ukraine.

Around the same time that T-64s began to appear in the hands of the DPR's armed formations in June 2014, numerous T-72s also began to turn up. These included more advanced models of T-72 including the T-72B Model 1989, which Ukraine did not possess at all. The T-72B Model 1989 differs significantly from the T-72B, being equipped with newer Kontakt-5 ERA, set in triangular shapes around the frontal turret arc, and on the glacis plate.

A notable 'local' DPR T-64 variant was paraded at the 9 May 2020 parade in Donetsk, in which displayed much more extensive Kontakt-1 ERA panels, covering all of the side skirts as well as a vastly enlarged turret bustle. Little is known about this DPR T-64 variant, and there was no evidence of it being used in action.

The situation with the T-72 tank presents an even clearer picture of direct Russian support to the DPR's armed formations. Ukraine inherited around 1,000 T-72B tanks from the Soviet Union but sold most of these in the years after gaining independence, choosing to base its armoured forces around the T-64 for the reasons noted above. By 2014, Ukraine had around 200 to 300 T-72s remaining, with these located in storage depots around Kyiv, far from Donbas.

During the battle of Ilovaisk in 2014, a T-72B3 destroyed by the Ukrainian armed forces was in use by the Russian armoured forces deployed to Ilovaisk at the time, rather than the DPR's armed formations.[11] The advanced T-72B3, only used by the Russian Army at the time of the battle, was widely used as evidence of direct Russian support to the DPR. This example is a classic case of the difficulty of unpicking the equipment and involvement of the DPR's armed formations and those of the Russian Federation, especially in an environment of intense information warfare on both sides.

Contrary to some claims, T-80 and T-90 tanks were not reliably documented in the possession of the DPR, nor were they ever paraded or publicly displayed. In a similar manner to the presence

A T-64BV bearing the flag of Somalia Battalion, parading through Donetsk on 9 May 2019. (Private photo collection, used with permission)

of the T-72B3 at the battle of Ilovaisk, T-90s spotted in Donbas in 2014 were in use by Russian Federation forces, thought to be the 136th Motorised Infantry Brigade.[12]

One much-publicised and highly unusual use of armoured vehicles by the DPR was the 'resurrection' of a plinth-mounted IS-3 heavy tank in 2014.[13] Located on a war memorial in the small village of Oleksandro-Kalynove, around 50km north of Donetsk, the tank was repaired and driven off the plinth by DPR militants on 5 July 2014.[14] Taken or driven to the nearby city of Kostiantynivka, it was painted with the Russian slogans 'To Kiev' and 'To Lvov' and fitted with a heavy machinegun, as the main armament was out of commission.

This IS-3 tank was abandoned in a tram depot when the Ukrainian ATO retook Kostiantynivka a few days later on 8 July 2014. Operationally its significance was minimal, but the propaganda value of this action to the DPR was far more valuable. The use of a Second World War-era tank (though the IS-3 did not actually see service before the war ended) in the 2014 conflict played well to the DPR's propaganda messaging around the Second World War and the victory over fascism. In Russia, a commemorative coin was issued relating to this event.

Infantry Fighting Vehicles and Armoured Personnel Carriers

BMP-1 and BMP-2 infantry fighting vehicles were in widespread use among all the DPR units. BMD-1 and BMD-2 airborne infantry fighting vehicles were also present, but in far fewer numbers. More modern BMP-3 infantry vehicles were not supplied via Kremlin 'voentorg.' Most BMP-1 or BMP-2s were used in standard configuration, with some being equipped with rubber side skirts or similar improvised armour.

The most interesting modification observed was presented in 2018, a BMP-2 displaying a comprehensive set of Kontakt-1 ERA blocks, including around the turret.[15] The vehicles shown displaying this armour were painted with a number 53 on the rear doors, suggesting affiliation with the 3rd Separate Motorised Rifle Brigade "Berkut".

In terms of armoured personnel carriers, the DPR made use of numerous tracked MT-LB and wheeled BTR-70 and BTR-80 APCs. Modernised versions of the BTR-80, supplied from the Russian Federation upgraded with Pl-1 laser illuminators and TKN-4GA-01 optical sights, were identified at DPR parades.[16]

Again, various modifications have been identified, with up-armoured MT-LBs making use of improvised side skirts, and one variant seen sporting a crude turret mounting a 2B9 Vasilek 82mm mortar system. The MT-LB was also used as a prime mover for towed artillery, as well as other uses.

One notable armoured vehicle identified in eastern Ukraine in use by the DPR was the armoured UAZ-23632-148 Esaul vehicle, the presence of which was first reliably confirmed in April 2021.[17] This vehicle is effectively a formalised version of the 'technicals' seen in conflicts in the Middle East. Built by the Russian company UAZ to include such features as armoured fuel tanks and a dedicated ring mount in the cargo bed for machine gun or automatic grenade launcher armament. At least 15 of these modern vehicles were thought to have been supplied to the DPR, to serve with rapid reaction forces able to deploy quickly along the contact line. Pushilin attended a handover ceremony in which the vehicles were presented to an unknown DPR armed formation unit.

Another feature of the DPR's utilisation of armoured vehicles was the use of them in roles other than that for which they were originally intended. The vast Soviet army of the 1970s and 1980s

Two T-72B main battle tanks parading through Donetsk on 9 May 2021. On the side of the tanks is a red star, an adaptation of the red, white and blue five-pointed star adopted as a symbol for the Russian Federation's military forces in 2014. (Private photo collection, used with permission)

A BMP-2 infantry fighting vehicle displayed by the DPR. The vehicle displays modifications, with neat side skirts fitted, handrails and steps for infantry dismounting, and an improvised attachment at the back of turret for storage. Donetsk, 9 May 2018. (Private photo collection, used with permission)

Older model trucks such as this Ural 375D, were utilised by the Internal Troops of the DPR's Ministry of Internal Affairs. Like all military trucks in the DPR, it bears a black number plate with white text, distinct from the white plates used by civilian vehicles. Donetsk, 2018 [Private photo collection, used with permission]

possessed numerous highly specialised vehicles, built to fight the Third World War in central Europe. These vehicles were now used in different and less specialised ways.

The BRDM-2RKh armoured car, constructed for nuclear and chemical reconnaissance, was used by the DPR's armed formations as a 'normal' scout/reconnaissance vehicle, even retaining its original flag dispensers. In another example, in the early stages of the conflict in Kramatorsk in 2014, the DPR attempted to use an IMR-2 armoured engineering vehicle to storm Kramatorsk airfield, which was held by Ukrainian forces.

A BRDM-2RKh armoured car, with flag dispenser at rear right. The number '15' in a circle denotes this BRDM-2RKh as being used by the DPR Separate Battalion of Command and Guard. Beyond is a KT-L recovery truck. Donetsk, 2019. (Private photo collection, used with permission)

Artillery

Artillery was perhaps the most important weapon possessed by the DPR armed formations, as it engaged in artillery duelling with Ukrainian units across the contact line. It was estimated that approximately 80 percent of all the casualties on both sides of the conflict were caused by artillery fire.[18]

The DPR was well-equipped with the 2S1 Gvozdika 122mm and 2S3 Akatsia 152mm self-propelled howitzers.[19] Kalmius Brigade possessed at least one 2S5 Giatsint-S 152mm self-propelled howitzer and one 2S19 Msta-S 152mm self-propelled howitzer, both captured from the Ukrainian armed forces.[20]

The 2S9 Nona 120mm self-propelled mortar was also reliably documented in use by the DPR, Vostok Regiment operated at least a couple of these, painted in an unusual brown/green camouflage pattern. Towed artillery was of a similar era, with the 2A18 D-30 122mm and 2A65 Msta-B 152mm towed howitzers common in the DPR's armed formations.

In terms of multiple launch rocket systems, variants of the BM-21 Grad 122mm MLRS were widespread, as well as sightings of the newer 2B26 system.[21] Kalmius operated at least a couple of the heavier BM-27 Uragan 220mm MLRS as well as associated transloaders. There is little evidence of DPR possession of the BM-30 Smerch MLRS 300mm MLRS, despite some claims to the contrary. BM-30 Smerch units photographed moving through Makiivka in late 2014 were far more likely to have been from a Russian Federation regular unit, deployed for a short period to the DPR to accomplish certain tasks.[22]

The TOS-1A Solntsepyok 220mm MLRS, designated a heavy flamethrower in Russian military nomenclature owing to its ability to fire thermobaric rockets, is also a weapon that is claimed by some analysts to be in the DPR's possession,[23] but even the highly active and pro-Ukrainian open-source investigative website InformNapalm was unable to find any conclusive visual proof of its presence in eastern Ukraine at any point from 2014-2022, let alone in the possession of the DPR.[24]

While there is significant witness testimony to suggest these systems were used in the 2014 fighting around Donetsk Airport, as with other more advanced and 'controversial' systems (i.e. those judged by the Kremlin as being more likely to indicate direct Russian involvement) they were most likely withdrawn after serving their purpose.

The DPR also developed a crude single launch rocket system, based upon 122mm 9M22 rockets usually fired by the BM-21 MLRS.[25] The rockets had undergone a certain degree of modification, including the fitting of static fins to stabilise the rocket in flight, and was fired from a single improvised launch cradle, angled towards the target. The system was dubbed the 'Chinese' – the name presumably referring to the superficial similarity between the system and the pictures of the earliest rockets fired from single launch rails in ancient China. In May 2017, the Ukrainian Azov Battalion posted a video depicting the results of a shelling of Krasnohorivka by the DPR, using 'Chinese' rockets.[26]

Air Defence Systems

In the early stages of the conflict in 2014, the Ukrainian armed forces were able to employ air power to considerable effect. In ground attack roles, Ukrainian Su-25 aircraft and attack helicopters were used at the First Battle of Donetsk Airport and helped to dislodge DPR and Russian forces from the terminal building.

2A65 Msta-B 152mm towed howitzers being paraded through Donetsk on 9 May 2021. (Private photo collection, used with permission)

A BM-21 Grad 122mm MLRS from Kalmius Brigade parades through Donetsk on 9 May 2021. (Private photo collection, used with permission)

Ukrainian transport aircraft like the Antonov An-26 were able to resupply Ukrainian forces across the region as the fighting escalated. Elsewhere, Ukrainian aircraft were used in an 'intimidation' role, such as the widely publicised flights of a heavily armed MiG-29 fighter aircraft which flew low passes over DPR forces in Kramatorsk and Sloviansk in April 2014.[27]

Initially, the DPR's armed formations had no answer to this airpower, other than the small arms available to them and heavy machine guns used in an anti-aircraft role. In these early stages of the conflict in 2014, Russia – though providing numerous other forms of massive military support including cross-border shelling – seemed unwilling to deploy its own airforce to provide air cover for the nascent DPR. The reason for this, it has been suggested, was that '...Russia could hardly dispatch its own air force, lest its plausible deniability of interfering in the country go up in smoke.'[28]

Instead, the DPR's armed formations began to receive supplies of air defence systems, starting with numerous Man-Portable Air Defence Systems (MANPADS) in the form of the 9K38 Igla and 9K32 Strela-2. It was quickly apparent that – though a small number

were captured from Ukrainian forces or stockpiles – the majority of supply was from Russia.

On 6 June 2014, Ukrainian forces '...recovered an empty munitions box for a 9M39 Igla man-portable, surface-to-air, air-defense missile in the village of Marynivka, approximately four kilometers from the Russian border. Official Russian-government records found in the container indicated that the missile belonged to the Russian Ministry of Defense, specifically a Russian military base near Rostov-on-Don, Russia.'[29]

On 18 May 2014, two launch tubes and the grip stock of the Polish-made Grom-E2 MANPADS (itself derived from the 9K38 Igla) were seized by Ukrainian forces belonging to the 8th Khmelnytsky Special Forces Regiment from DPR militants in Kramatorsk. It emerged that this particular weapons system had most likely been captured from Georgian forces by the Russian military during the 2008 war in Georgia. It was an example of how far the Kremlin was keen to go in the initial phases of the conflict in Donbas to obfuscate its involvement in the transfer of weaponry.

The venerable ZU-23-2 23mm towed anti-aircraft cannon also came into widespread use, mounted in static fortifications or mobile on trucks and MT-LBs, though generally utilised in a ground-to-ground role.

Towards the middle of 2014, more advanced anti-aircraft systems began to appear in the DPR. The most visible system, in a propaganda sense, was the 9K35 Strela-10, paraded yearly in Donetsk on 9 May, comprised a highly mobile anti-aircraft system mounted on a modified MT-LB tracked chassis. It soon became commonplace across the DPR armed formations, in which '...all brigades have organic air-defence elements, composed of a few Strela-10 … vehicles.'[30]

The wheeled 9K33 Osa air defence system was also documented in the possession of the DPR.[31] Unlike the 9K35 Strela, much less emphasis is placed in public on this system in DPR use, and it has not been paraded.

Backing the DPR's deployment of these air defence assets was the use of air defence radars strategically spaced across the territory of the DPR. Set in place after the relative 'stabilisation' of the front line after the capture of Debaltseve, the radars provided a means of early warning against aerial attack. Evidently linked to form an integrated air defence system, the radars were in place for so long in some locations that the systems themselves and their defensive earthworks were easily visible on commercially available satellite imagery.[32]

These radars were Soviet-era P-15 or P-19 surveillance and target acquisition radars, one based near the town of Rozivka and one near Mospyne. No known fixed radar station inside the DPR has been identified south of Mospyne. Further stations in LPR-held territory to the north-east, set at a similar distance of some 20-30km from the contact line, completed this chain of radars.

Air defence was a key area where there was likely close integration with regular Russian Federation forces, and the Ukrainian military also reported the occasional flying of Beriev A-50 early warning and control aircraft up and down the border in Rostov oblast. Such

'Russian Charitable Aviation – Rooks Without Borders' morale patch. The patch is a wordplay in Russian: The Su-25 ground attack aircraft is nicknamed the 'Rook' ('Grach' in Russian), and the phrase 'Грачи без границ / Grachi bez granits' is a play on words for the international NGO Doctors Without Borders ('Врачи без границ / Vrachi Bez Granits' in Russian). At the time, MSF hospitals in Syria were being repeatedly struck by Russian and Syrian airstrikes. Morale patch, widely available in Donetsk, c. 2016. (Author's collection)

aircraft would have been able to cover most of the area controlled by the DPR, without leaving Russian airspace.

The lack of more widespread and sophisticated air defence systems, given the potential overwhelming air superiority of the Ukrainian Air Force, was the result of a combination of factors. Among these may have been the international outrage caused by the shooting down of Malaysian Airlines MH17 on 17 July 2014, most probably by a 9K37 Buk system fired from DPR-controlled territory near the town of Snizhne.[33]

A ZU-23-2 23mm anti-aircraft cannon mounted on a Ural 43206, parading on 9 May 2018, Donetsk. The militants sitting by the cannon are wearing the 'dogs head' patches of the DPR Separate Commandant's Regiment. (Private photo collection, used with permission)

A 9K35 Strela-10 being paraded through Donetsk on 9 May 2018. To the right of the vehicle, people in the crowd hold up photos of relatives who participated in the Second World War or the ongoing conflict in Donbas, part of the 'Immortal Regiment' commemorative movement. (Private photo collection, used with permission)

While senior DPR leaders like Borodai and Zakharchenko steadfastly maintained that the DPR had not been involved in the downing of MH17,[34] in an interview with Reuters, the commander of Vostok, Khodakovsky, noted that a Buk system had been in the DPR at the time, having crossed over the border from LPR-controlled areas in Luhansk oblast.[35]

The subsequent rapid disappearance of this system was evidently an attempt to limit reputational damage to the DPR and Russia and was combined with the promotion of various 'competing theories' about how the tragedy occurred in an attempt to shift blame. Since the shooting down of MH17, no 9K37 Buk systems, or indeed any air defence systems more advanced or capable than the 9K35 Strela-10, were claimed or openly paraded by the DPR.

The rapid expansion of the DPR's anti-aircraft capabilities over the summer of 2014 had a profound effect on the direction of the conflict. Initially able to leverage its air superiority for close air support, reconnaissance and resupply, the initial phases of Ukraine's ATO were able to steadily reverse the DPR's territorial gains. However, as the summer of 2014 wore on, there were steadily increasing losses of Ukrainian aircraft to DPR MANPADS and air defence systems. In August 2014 for example, one Ukrainian MiG-29 was shot down over Yenakiieve, and one Su-25 over the small town of Starobesheve, south of Donetsk.

These mounting losses effectively caused the cessation of Ukrainian combat flights over DPR-controlled areas in Donbas in August 2014, and the threat to the DPR's armed formations from Ukrainian fixed and rotary wing crewed combat aircraft was in this way negated.

However, as the conflict progressed, the use of UAVs by both sides increased exponentially, culminating in the use by the Ukrainian armed forces in October 2021 of a Turkish-made Bayraktar TB-2 UAV to strike a DPR D-30 artillery position in the southern part of DPR-controlled territory.[36] The traditional and mostly Soviet-era air defence systems built up by the DPR were much less effective against smaller UAVs, which will be discussed in greater detail below.

Aircraft

One notable absence in the armoury of the two People's Republics in eastern Ukraine is the total lack of any form of traditional crewed aircraft, either fixed-wing or rotary. The Minsk Agreements stipulated a 'no fly' zone, but – given the flagrant violations of the Minsk Agreements by the DPR in other weapon class areas – the lack of aircraft supplied to the DPR was likely owing to an analysis of the situation on the ground.

Effective and numerous Ukrainian air defence systems, lack of trained pilots, and high maintenance and running costs may have factored in to the decision not to provide the DPR armed formations with any form of crewed aerial units.

Indeed, since the first year of the conflict, which saw the loss of a number of Ukrainian Air Force aircraft to MANPADs and other air defence systems (discussed above), neither side used any crewed aircraft in the skies directly above the contact line, for either reconnaissance or offensive operations.

The DPR displayed a small Aero L-29 Delfin jet trainer aircraft in DPR colours at the 2018 9 May Parade, but this was purely for propaganda purposes, and most likely a leftover from a civilian flying club.

An Aero L-29 Delfin jet trainer at the 2018 9 May parade in Donetsk. Such a display was purely for propaganda purposes. (Private photo collection, used with permission)

UAVs

As the conflict developed, and in particular after the front lines mostly stabilised after early 2015, the use of UAVs gained increasing prominence in the conflict in Donbas, as tools for reconnaissance, artillery fire correction, and also as a means of delivering ordnance onto targets. In keeping with broader trends in contemporaneous modern conflict, the use of UAVs escalated as a means of providing forms of air power that did not require huge investment in traditional fleets of aircraft, which as discussed above were not available to the DPR.

Underscoring the volunteer and often amateur nature of the initial armed formations formed by the DPR, the use of UAVs was hampered by training issues. One DPR commander, interviewed by Matveeva, noted that: 'We brought the first drone which flew for 20 km, not any worse than those the Ukrainians had. Then we discovered that it was lying idle because nobody could read instructions in English. We had to look for a person in Russia who could come to teach the locals how to use it.'[37]

Already by August 2014 the DPR had formed a unit called the 1st Separate Aviation Squadron "Grenada" which operated small commercial quadcopters and a small hobbyist fixed-wing UAV.[38] Apparently the first UAV lost by the unit was brought down by friendly fire from Vostok Battalion.

UAVs used by the DPR broadly fell into three categories: off the shelf commercial models, Russian made military UAVs, and a small number of UAVs supposedly made in the DPR. Commercial quadcopter drones were probably the most widely used, being cheap and widely available. As well as the obvious reconnaissance and target correction roles performed by such UAVs, the DPR was able to weaponise such commercial drones, using them to drop hand grenades and other small munitions onto Ukrainian positions.[39]

In one such incident on 13 April 2021, DPR armed formations located in the Horlivka area utilised a commercial UAV in the early morning hours to drop a POM-2 anti-personnel mine on a UAF position at the Maiorsk crossing point, used by civilians to

cross the contact line.[40] The mine was neutralised by the Ukrainian armed forces.

From 2014 to 2022, numerous Russian Federation-made military drones were also identified in Donbas, these included the Granat-1, Granat-2, Granat-4, Forpost, Orlan-10, Eleron-3SV, Zastava, and Tachyon systems.[41] However, the extent to which these more advanced UAVs were actually used by the DPR, as opposed to Russian Federation forces embedded with the DPR, is a matter for debate. Some Ukrainian observers thought it likely that the majority of these UAVs were utilised by Russian Federation reconnaissance elements deployed in Donbas.[42] However, there is open-source intelligence suggesting the formal transfer of Orlan-10, Tachyon and Eleron UAVs to the DPR.[43]

Lastly, the DPR demonstrated a limited number of UAVs supposedly made in the DPR itself, in keeping for its desire to be seen developing its own weaponry, a trend discussed further below. In keeping with this, the DPR displayed for the first time a number of small, fixed-wing UAVs during the 2021 Victory Day parade.

In the 2021 Victory Parade, a number of systems were carried past the crowds on the back of Ural trucks. One was clearly a Ukrainian-made PD-2 reconnaissance UAV, though it was unclear if it was being paraded as 'captured equipment' or as one now in use by the DPR itself. Two other small fixed-wing UAVs were present, on launching ramps, suggesting operational systems.

A fixed-wing UAV was also displayed in the 2018 parade as a system 'made in the DPR,' but it was clearly a very crude affair, and there is little evidence of it being used in combat – or even flown at all.

The widespread use of UAVs in the conflict in Donbas also lead to the development of increasingly sophisticated decoys by both sides, including dummy positions and vehicles. Dummy figures carrying old RPG tubes or wooden weapons – so-called 'scarecrow soldiers' – were also a common sight at DPR positions on the contact line, including at the crossing points.

A Ukrainian-made PD-2 reconnaissance UAV, being paraded by the DPR through Donetsk on 9 May 2021. This example was still painted in the characteristic digital camouflage pattern utilised by the Ukrainian armed forces. (Private photo collection, used with permission)

Electronic Warfare

The presence of advanced Russian Federation electronic warfare equipment in Ukraine has been well documented. At the 2015 battle for Debaltseve, R-330Zh Zhitel systems were used to jam Ukrainian communications, hampering the Ukrainian defence of the city and contributing to the eventual capture of the city by combined DPR, LPR and Russian forces.

As the importance of UAVs in the conflict grew in the years after 2015, the use of electronic warfare systems developed in proportion. For the DPR armed formations, the means of disrupting Ukrainian UAVs became increasingly important, especially as they had limited means of countering small commercial UAVs other than small arms fire.

Forms of electronic jamming, and GPS jamming or spoofing, slowly became prevalent across the contact line area, in particular around the known 'flashpoints.'

The Russian Federation evidently used the Donbas as a testing ground for new systems, and over time other advanced electronic warfare systems were identified in the region, including the RB-341V Leer-3 and RB-636 Svet-KU.[44]

Other than very vague references to a DPR 'Electronic Warfare Company,' there is very little evidence to suggest that the DPR directly operated any of these electronic warfare systems, and this is an area where the Russian Federation likely deployed such assets and operated them directly, in liaison with and in support of DPR armed formations in the area.

Trucks and Light Vehicles

While a lot of attention and analysis was paid over the years to the more obvious 'flag' equipment supplied to the DPR by the Russian Federation, less attention was given to the military trucks used by the DPR's armed formations.

One of the most common trucks seen in use by the DPR armed formations was a newer version of the Ural-4320 6x6 truck mounting an updated YaMZ engine, easily identified by an enlarged engine compartment and large black cylindrical air filter on the passenger side of the bonnet. Various other features distinguished it from the older, Soviet-era Urals widely used by the Ukrainian armed forces.

These new versions of the Ural-4320 truck were never supplied to the Ukrainian armed forces and appeared in large numbers in the

This photograph shows what appears to be a PKTM machine gun on a locally made improvised mount for use against drones and UAVs. (Photograph by Dean O'Brien)

hands of the DPR's armed formations. An even newer 4x4 variant, the Ural-43206, was even easier to distinguish having one axle fewer, and was seen in widespread use by the Vostok Battalion, for example.

In a similar vein, a recent Conflict Armament Research report examined several KamAZ-5350 trucks seized by the Ukrainian armed forces from the armed formations, with dates of manufacture in the 2000s.[45]

In terms of light vehicles, standard Soviet-era light vehicle types like the UAZ-469 light utility vehicle were ubiquitous. Interestingly, and in keeping with the restricted nature of supply to the DPR, though modern military trucks like the aforementioned Ural-43206 were widely disseminated to the DPR, other common Russian Federation military utility vehicles like the GAZ Tigr and

A Ural-43206 truck in use by the DPR. The number '55' in a triangle on the door indicates the truck is associated with Oplot Brigade. Makiivka, 2018. (Private photo collection, used with permission)

its armoured sub-variants were not seen in Donbas except in very limited numbers and most likely belonging to regular Russian units.

An unusual vehicle observed in use by Vostok Battalion and other armed formation units was the amphibious LuAZ-967 utility vehicle. Built in Lutsk in western Ukraine for Soviet airborne troops from the 1960s to the late 1980s, the lightweight LuAZ-967 saw action in Donbas on both sides of the contact line.

Self-Developed Weaponry

One notable aspect of the weaponry in use by the DPR was the development, for a period from around 2017-2018, of self-made weaponry that was publicly put on display at the 2018 9 May parade in Donetsk.[46]

The two most prominent systems were two completely unique MLRS vehicles. The first was called 'Snezhinka' (Snowflake), based on a 6x6 KrAZ truck chassis and mounting two 324mm unguided rockets.[47] The second MLRS was called 'Cheburashka' (named after a famous Soviet-era children's character), also on a 6x6 KrAZ chassis, and firing 217mm rockets from a total of 64 tubes arrayed in two 'packs.'[48] While some online commentators immediately attacked the relative crudeness of these systems, there is video evidence of them being successfully test fired. As a side note, the DPR-made 'Chinese' rockets noted in the MLRS section above were not displayed at the 2018 parade.

Other weaponry on display at the same parade included a small remote weapons station mounting a machine gun, and a so-called 'anti-sniper' gun called the 'Separatist', chambered for the same 23mm cannon round as the ZU-23-2 anti-aircraft gun, and weighing a reported 44kg. However, in this case there is no open-source evidence to show it actually being test fired, let alone used in combat.[49]

There were also some mortars, a variety of small arms, and other minor equipment on display. An unnamed UAV was also presented, but it appeared to be fairly crude, and there is little evidence of it being used or progressing to production phase.

All these items were reported to have been developed by the so-called 'Military-Industrial Complex' of the DPR, reportedly an agglomeration of various machine-building plants on the areas under the DPR's control and commanded at the time by the then Deputy Prime Minister of the DPR, Alexander Timofeev.

However, the development of such systems raises questions about the nature of the proxy-benefactor relationship, and why such weapons development was even deemed necessary in the context of a potentially almost inexhaustible supply of weapons and ammunition of and for existing types from the Russian Federation.

Pro-Ukrainian observers tend to point to a theory of 'legalisation' or 'legitimisation' of Russian Federation weaponry in the hands of the People's Republics, however this seems unlikely given the development of quite visibly distinct types of weaponry and ammunition: the supply of Soviet-era weapons systems which could plausibly have been captured from Ukrainian forces or stockpiles meets the 'legitimisation' argument better.

The development of such weaponry, which even sympathetic Russian websites pointed out as being quite crude, pointed more to dynamics within the DPR and in particular its desire to be seen as a potentially independent political unit. Even the choice of modern KrAZ platforms to mount the two MLRS could have been a pointed 'political' statement, as in the Ukrainian conflict variants of KrAZ trucks were in heavy use by the Ukrainian armed forces as the KrAZ company was headquartered in Kremenchuk in central Ukraine. The DPR, as noted above, in general made much heavier use of the Ural and KamAZ truck platforms.

A Ural-43206 moving at speed through civilian traffic. The unit number on the door has been obscured with masking tape, possibly indicating a Russian military truck making a journey to a destination in the DPR. The extended engine compartment and large air filter of the newer YaMZ engines are clearly visible here. Makiivka 2018. (Private collection, used with permission)

Notably, after the death of Alexander Zakharchenko in August 2018, in an explosion that also wounded Alexander Timofeev (who subsequently was removed from post and moved to Russia), the development of DPR weaponry was not as prominently discussed or openly touted.

Uniforms and Kit

From the early rag-tag assembly of uniforms and kit that DPR militants wore in the first stages of the conflict in 2014, the uniforms used by the armed formations slowly became more regular as

Two of the most unusual weapons systems developed by the DPR. In the foreground is the MLRS system 'Snezhinka' equipped with two 324mm unguided rockets (the rockets here mock-ups for parade purposes), and on the left is the 'Cheburashka' system. In the background are the domes of the Holy Transfiguration Cathedral. Donetsk, 9 May 2018. (Private photo collection, used with permission)

The DPR-made 23mm 'Separatist' anti-materiel rifle, on display at an exhibition of DPR weaponry. Donetsk, 9 May 2018. (Private photo collection, used with permission)

Arbuz patterns also being common. As the DPR's armed formations became more formalised, uniforms based on the 2008 Russian EMR 'digital flora' pattern became standard, in the normal 'summer' variant. For winter wear, the Gorka suit was prevalent, as well as snow camouflage patterns based around the *klyaksa* (ink blot) pattern.

Despite extensive supply of EMR uniforms however, a staggering display of camouflage patterns, both military surplus and commercial, remained common across the DPR armed formations. These included genuine combat uniforms most likely obtained from military surplus, including German Fleckentarn, as well as numerous 'commercial' camouflage patterns.

the armed formations underwent reorganisation, resupply and 'formalisation'.

Soviet-era camouflage patterns predominated in early armed formation units, with variants of the 1970s-era 'sun ray' camouflage uniform (favoured by Sparta Battalion), and the 1990s Flora or

Khodakovsky was frequently pictured wearing American-pattern MultiCam uniforms, for example, with the Vostok Brigade patch on his arm. Another use of what might be considered unusual camouflage patterns included the widespread utilisation of classic British DPM worn by DPR armed formation units including Republican Guard and the MGB.

This soldier of the Vostok Battalion wears what appears to be a Russian ZSH-1 helmet and SUMRAK lightweight/summer uniform in Multicam. (Photograph by Dean O'Brien)

Away from the neat uniforms displayed on parades, DPR armed formation militants wore a wide variety of combat uniforms. This is probably a commercial variant. The ubiquitous AK-74M is also visible. 2021. (Private photo collection, used with permission)

10
MEDALS AND MEMORIALISATION

As with other unrecognised states around the world, the DPR created a complex system of military awards, as well as means of memorialising fallen militants. Broadly speaking, as will be discussed below, the system of medals and broader memorialisation closely followed Soviet traditions.

Medals

The highest award conferred by the DPR was the Gold Star Hero of the Donetsk People's Republic medal, which is represented by a gold star under a ribbon comprised of the DPR colours: black, blue and red. The first medal was awarded in 2014 to Vladimir Kononov, who was the Minister of Defence of the DPR. Subsequent awards were made to individuals including Alexander Zakharchenko, as well as other high-profile DPR unit commanders. The design of the medal is effectively a copy of the Hero of the Soviet Union award, with the red Soviet ribbon replaced, as noted, with the DPR tricolour.

The DPR also issued four 'For the Defence of' medals, awarded to those who participated in the battles for these four cities during the first year of the war. In general concept and design, the DPR 'For the Defence of' medals mirrored that of the eight Soviet defence medals issued during the Second World War, which were awarded to those who participated in the defence of cities such as Leningrad, Moscow and Stalingrad.

The Gold Star Hero of the Donetsk People's Republic medal. The award was created on 3 October 2014. Postcard no. 1 in the set 'Gold Star Heroes', issued by the DPR Ministry of Communication, 2017. (Author's collection)

The medals were 'For the Defence of Slavyansk' for those who fought in the city of Sloviansk in 2014, 'For the Defence of Saur-Mogila,' 'For the Defence of Shakhtyorsk,' and 'For the Defence of Ilovaisk' awarded to DPR participants in the battle for that city.

Memorialisation

As noted, a main theme of the DPR's propaganda and symbology was creating a seamless continuation in the minds of the populace between the Great Patriotic War of 1941-45, and the conflict in Donbas. In keeping with this, halls at Donetsk's Museum of the Great Patriotic War were given over to the conflict in Donbas, with small display cases displaying the personal effects of fallen fighters, and scale models of important battles in the DPR's founding mythology, such as Savur-Mohyla.[1]

Another way of commemorating fighters was by the use of star-shaped plaques on houses, which noted that a 'Hero of the DPR lives here.' This is a method of commemoration that borrowed directly from the post-1945 Soviet Union, where plaques on gates and houses proclaimed that a 'Participant in the Great Patriotic War lives here.'

Public Holidays

Just as the DPR rejected the 'decommunization' drive decreed by the Ukrainian government, it maintained a different set of public holidays. The importance of the 9 May Victory parade has already been discussed above, another holiday observed by the DPR was 23 February.

Originating in the Soviet Union in 1919, it marked the day the first mass conscriptions were made into the Red Army. Undergoing a series of name changes over the decades, it survived in post-Soviet Russia as Defender of the Fatherland Day. In Ukraine after independence, the holiday was not officially observed, and in 2014 a new holiday called Defender of Ukraine Day was instigated annually on 14 October.

The DPR reinstated 23 February as Defender of the Fatherland Day, observing this holiday and, as with the 9 May celebrations, utilising a blend of old and new imagery to create a visual spectacle around the day.

'Awards await heroes!' These are in fact all imaginary medals, from left to right: 'For the Defence of Slavyansk' (a medal the DPR did issue, but not in this form), 'For the Liberation of Kiev' and 'For the Taking of Lvov.' Magnet, c. 2016. (Author's collection)

'On the Day of Liberation of Donbass!' DPR visual propaganda heavily favoured the art of photomontage, here blending a Second World War Soviet photo with that of DPR militants, in this case from Slavyansk Brigade. Donetsk, date unknown. (Private photo collection, used with permission)

Defender of the Fatherland Day poster. Olenivka, February 2018. (Private photo collection, used with permission)

DPR Defender of the Fatherland Day stamp and first day envelope. First day envelope issued on 23 February 2019. A DPR T-64BV main battle tank is depicted on the stamp. (Author's collection)

11
CONCLUSION

This book has highlighted how from their creation in 2014 the DPR's armed formations, eventually formed into DPR 1st Army Corps, underwent eight years of development as the Kremlin's major proxy in eastern Ukraine.

The motivations of the DPR militants fighting the Ukrainian state varied widely, and the goals of DPR leaders and senior commanders were diffuse and often unclear. The Kremlin, in turn, seemed to vacillate between varying degrees of support, in stark contrast to the rapid and confident manner with which Crimea had been annexed in 2014.

From this uncertainty stemmed the violent chaos and factional infighting that plagued both People's Republics from the start. From 2014 the DPR occupied a space in eastern Ukraine which operated outside the norms of international rule of law that govern truly sovereign states. Inside this unrecognised state, the DPR leadership ruled by a monopoly on violence, thinly concealed beneath the trappings of an imitation democracy. As one Russian critic of the Kremlin's policy in Donbas scathingly wrote: 'On the territories controlled by the separatists, total de-modernization has taken place. Archaic tribal practices rule; the strong hold all the rights;

there's the law of the Kalashnikov ... It's not surprising that the Lugansk and Donetsk Peoples' Republics have together earned the nickname ... of "Luganda."'[1]

As noted in the introduction, this book is intended as historical, rather than predictive, an attempt to record the way the Kremlin initiated the conflict in Donbas in 2014, and the form taken by and capabilities of its heavily armed proxy, the DPR 1st Army Corps.

On 24 February 2022, Putin's massive 'special military operation' began, with one of its goals to compel Ukraine to recognise the independence of the DPR and LPR within the pre-2014 Donetsk and Luhansk oblast boundaries to which each People's Republic had respectively laid claim.

The majority of the DPR 1st Army Corps units described in this book were – at the time of writing – fully engaged in this campaign, with some advancing alongside Russian Federation forces towards Mariupol and Volnovakha. The outcome of the conflict will very much determine not just the future of the DPR and LPR as political entities, but reshape the security architecture of the whole of Europe.

BIBLIOGRAPHY

Books

Allan, Duncan, *The Minsk Conundrum: Western Policy and Russia's War in Eastern Ukraine* (London: Chatham House, 2020)

Anon, *Weapons of the War in Ukraine: A three-year investigation of weapon supplies into Donetsk and Luhansk* (Conflict Armament Research, 2021) https://www.conflictarm.com/reports/weapons-of-the-war-in-ukraine/

Caspersen, Nina, *Unrecognized States* (Cambridge: Polity, 2012)

Chivers, Christopher J., *The Gun: The Story of the AK-47* (London: Penguin, 2011)

Clover, Charles, *Black Wind, White Snow – The rise of Russia's new nationalism* (New Haven: Yale University Press, 2016)

D'Anieri, Paul, *Russia and Ukraine – From civilized divorce to uncivil war* (Cambridge: Cambridge University Press, 2019)

Davis, Vicky, *Myth Making in the Soviet Union and Modern Russia – Remembering World War II in Brezhnev's Hero City* (London: Bloomsbury, 2020)

de Waal, Thomas and von Twickel, Nikolaus, *Beyond Frozen Conflict – Scenarios for the separatist disputes of Eastern Europe* (London: Centre for European Policy Studies, 2020)

Ferguson, Jonathan and Jenzen-Jones, N. R., *Raising Red Flags: An Examination of Arms and Munitions in the Ongoing Conflict in Ukraine* (ARES, 2014)

Freedman, Lawrence, *Ukraine and the Art of Strategy* (Oxford: Oxford University Press, 2019)

Galeotti, Mark, *Armies of Russia's War in Ukraine* (Oxford: Osprey, 2019)

Judah, Tim, *In Wartime: Stories from Ukraine* (London: Penguin, 2016)

Kofman, Michael, Migacheva, Katya, Nichiporuk, Brian, Radin, Andrew, Tkacheva, Olesya and Oberholtzer, Jenny, *Lessons from Russia's Operations in Crimea and Eastern Ukraine* (Santa Monica: RAND Corporation, 2017)

Kuzio, Taras, *Putin's War Against Ukraine – Revolution, Nationalism, and Crime* (CreateSpace Independent Publishing Platform, 2017), ISBN 978-1543285864, p.21

Matveeva, Anna, *Through Times of Trouble – Conflict in Southeastern Ukraine Explained from Within* (Lanham: Lexington Books, 2018)

Medvedev, Sergei, *The Return of the Russian Leviathan* (Cambridge: Polity Press, 2020)

Mumford, Andrew, *Proxy Warfare* (Cambridge: Polity Press, 2013)

Menon, Rajan and Rumer, Eugene, *Conflict in Ukraine – The unwinding of the post-Cold War order* (Cambridge, Mass.: The MIT Press, 2015)

Miller, James, Vaux, Pierre, Fitzpatrick, Catherine A. and Weiss, Michael, *An Invasion by Any Other Name: The Kremlin's Dirty War in Ukraine* (New York: Frontline Printing, 2015)

Pieniążek, Paweł, *Greetings from Novorossiya: Eyewitness to the War in Ukraine* (Pittsburgh: University of Pittsburgh Press, 2017)

Renz, Bettina and Smith, Hanna, *Russia and hybrid warfare: Going beyond the label* (Helsinki: Kikimora Publications at the Aleksanteri Institute, University of Helsinki, Finland, 2016)

Sakwa, Richard, *Frontline Ukraine – Crisis in the borderlands* (London: I B Tauris, 2014)

Shevchenko, Artem, *Slovyansk: The Beginning of the War* (Folio, 2020), ISBN 978-9660394155

Sutyagin, Igor and Bronk, Justin, *Russia's New Ground Forces: Capabilities, Limitations and Implications for International Security* (Abingdon: Routledge, 2017)

Swain, Adam (ed.), *Re-constructing the Post-Soviet Industrial Region: The Donbas in transition* (Caombridge: Cambridge University Press, 2007)

Toal, Gerard, *Near Abroad – Putin, the West, and the contest over Ukraine and the Caucasus* (Oxford: Oxford University Press, 2017)

Walker, Shaun, *The Long Hangover: Putin's New Russia and the Ghosts of the Past* (New York: Oxford University Press USA, 2018)

Wood, Tony, *Russia Without Putin: Money, Power and the Myths of the New Cold War* (London: Verso, 2018)

Yaffa, Joshua, *Between Two Fires – Truth, ambition and compromise in Putin's Russia* (London: Granta, 2020)(uncorrected bound proof, Jan 2020)

Yekelchyk, Serhy, *The Conflict in Ukraine* (Oxford: Oxford University Press, 2015)

Journal Articles

Abibok, Yulia, 'On the way to creating the 'Donbas people' – Identity policy in the self-proclaimed republics in east Ukraine', *OSW Commentary*, number 270 (June 2018)

Anon, 'Peace in Ukraine (III): The Costs of War in Donbas', International Crisis Group, Report No. 261 (3 Sept 2020), https://www.crisisgroup.org/europe-central-asia/eastern-europe/ukraine/261-peace-ukraine-iii-costs-war-donbas

Дурнев, Дмитрий, 'Карта акторов конфликта на Донбассе: локальные акторы ОРДО' (CivilM+ 2020)

Kolstø, Pål, 'Crimea vs. Donbas: How Putin Won Russian Nationalist Support—and Lost it Again', *Slavic Review* 75, no. 3 (Fall 2016)

Kolstø, Pål, 'Symbol of the War — But Which One? The St George Ribbon in Russian Nation Building', *The Slavonic and East European Review*, Vol. 94, No. 4 (October 2016), pp.665–666, https://doi.org/10.5699/slaveasteurorev2.94.4.0660

Laruelle, Marlene, 'The three colors of Novorossiya, or the Russian nationalist mythmaking of the Ukrainian crisis', *Post-Soviet Affairs*, 32:1 (2016), pp.55–74, DOI: 10.1080/1060586X.2015.1023004

Loshkariov, Ivan D., and Sushentsov, Andrey A., 'Radicalization of Russians in Ukraine: from 'accidental' diaspora to rebel movement', *Southeast European and Black Sea Studies*, 16:1 (2016), pp.71–90, DOI: 10.1080/14683857.2016.1149349

Malyarenko, Tetyana and Galbreath, David J., Paramilitary motivation in Ukraine: beyond integration and abolition, *Southeast European and Black Sea Studies*, 16:1 (2016), pp.113–138, DOI: 10.1080/14683857.2016.1148414

Matveeva, Anna, 'No Moscow stooges: identity polarization and guerrilla movements in Donbass', *Southeast European and Black Sea Studies*, 16:1 (2016), pp.25–50, DOI:10.1080/14683857.2016.1148415

Noorman, Randy, 'The Battle of Debaltseve: a Hybrid Army in a Classic Battle of Encirclement', *Small Wars Journal*, 17 July 2020, https://smallwarsjournal.com/jrnl/art/battle-debaltseve-hybrid-army-classic-battle-encirclement

NOTES

Introduction and Acknowledgements

1   Andrew Mumford, *Proxy Warfare* (Cambridge: Polity Press, 2013), chapter 1.

2   Gerard Toal, *Near Abroad – Putin, the West, and the contest over Ukraine and the Caucasus* (Oxford: Oxford University Press, 2017), p.20.

3   Tetyana Malyarenko and David J. Galbreath, 'Paramilitary motivation in Ukraine: beyond integration and abolition', *Southeast European and Black Sea Studies*, 16:1 (2016), pp.113–138, DOI: 10.1080/14683857.2016.1148414; p.115.

4   Address by the President of the Russian Federation, 24 February 2022.

5   As an example: 'Rhetoric is changed in ORDiLO', *Ukrainian Week* website, 2019, https://ukrainianweek.com/Society/232471.

6   Oblast – the first unit of territorial sub-division in Ukraine, roughly equivalent to a UK county or US state.

7   Nina Caspersen, *Unrecognized States* (Cambridge: Polity, 2012), p.6.

8   Yulia Abibok, 'On the way to creating the 'Donbas people' – Identity policy in the self-proclaimed republics in east Ukraine', *OSW Commentary*, number 270 (June 2018), p.6.

9   Lanre Bakare, 'The force awakens (in Ukraine): Darth Vader statue replaces Lenin monument', *Guardian* website (23 October 2015), https://www.theguardian.com/film/2015/oct/23/darth-vader-statue-erected-ukraine.

10   This difference in spelling originates in the differing transliterations from Ukrainian and Russian. Similar differences are observed in the spelling of the Ukrainian capital Kyiv (Ukrainian language) vs Kiev (Russian language); and Odesa (Ukrainian language) vs Odessa (Russian language).

Chapter 1

1   Serhy Yekelchyk, *The Conflict in Ukraine* (Oxford: Oxford University Press, 2015), p.5.

2   Paul D'Anieri, *Russia and Ukraine – From civilized divorce to uncivil war* (Cambridge: Cambridge University Press 2019), pp.2–3.

3   'Bucharest Summit Declaration – Issued by the Heads of State and Government participating in the meeting of the North Atlantic Council in Bucharest on 3 April 2008', NATO website, https://www.nato.int/cps/en/natolive/official_texts_8443.htm.

4   'Vladimir Putin tells summit he wants security and friendship', *The Times*, 5 April 2008.

5   Rajan Menon and Eugene Rumer, *Conflict in Ukraine – The unwinding of the post-Cold War order* (Cambridge, Mass.: The MIT Press, 2015), p.11.

6   Adam Swain (ed.), *Re-constructing the Post-Soviet Industrial Region: The Donbas in transition* (Cambridge: Cambridge University Press 2007).

7   Abibok, 'On the way to creating the 'Donbas people' – Identity policy in the self-proclaimed republics in east Ukraine', p.2.

8   Abibok, 'On the way to creating the 'Donbas people' – Identity policy in the self-proclaimed republics in east Ukraine', p.3.

9   Malyarenko and Galbreath, 'Paramilitary motivation in Ukraine', p.128.

10   Mark Galeotti, *Armies of Russia's War in Ukraine* (Oxford: Osprey 2019), pp.12–14.

11   Thomas de Waal and Nikolaus von Twickel, *Beyond Frozen Conflict – Scenarios for the separatist disputes of Eastern Europe* (London: Centre for European Policy Studies, 2020), p.64.

12   Khodakovsky, quoted in an interview with Shaun Walker, *The Long Hangover: Putin's New Russia and the Ghosts of the Past* (New York: Oxford University Press USA, 2018), p.199.

Chapter 2

1   'Пушилин подписал приказ о всеобщей мобилизации', DAN News website, 19 Feb 2022, https://dan-news.info/politics/pushilin-podpisal-prikaz-o-vseobschej-mobilizacii/

2   Anna Matveeva, *Through Times of Trouble – Conflict in Southeastern Ukraine Explained from Within* (Lanham: Lexington Books, 2018), pp.98–99.

3   Jorge A Rodriguez, 'Eight Spaniards arrested after returning from combat in Ukraine', *El Pais* website; 27 Feb 2015, https://english.elpais.com/elpais/2015/02/27/inenglish/1425033238_750840.html

4   Matveeva, *Through Times of Trouble – Conflict in Southeastern Ukraine Explained from Within*, p.99.

5   Marlene Laruelle, 'The three colors of Novorossiya, or the Russian nationalist mythmaking of the Ukrainian crisis', *Post-Soviet Affairs* (2016), 32:1, DOI: 10.1080/1060586X.2015.1023004, pp.55–74.

6   Ivan D. Loshkariov and Andrey A. Sushentsov, 'Radicalization of Russians in Ukraine: from 'accidental' diaspora to rebel movement', *Southeast European and Black Sea Studies*, 16:1 (2016), pp.71–90, DOI: 10.1080/14683857.2016.1149349, p.79.

7   For an example YouTube video, see: 'Украина: 300 Стрелковцев', YouTube website, 21 September 2014, https://www.youtube.com/watch?v=QL5IH_ODWac

8   Pål Kolstø, 'Symbol of the War — But Which One? The St George Ribbon in Russian Nation-Building', *The Slavonic and East European Review*, Vol. 94, No. 4 (October 2016), pp.665–666, https://doi.org/10.5699/slaveasteurorev2.94.4.0660

9   Matveeva, *Through Times of Trouble – Conflict in Southeastern Ukraine Explained from Within*, p.79.

10   Now the city of Krivy-Rih in Ukraine. To this day the location of vast deposits of iron ore, it was the linking of the cities of Donetsk and Krivy-Rih by railway in the late nineteenth century that helped create the vast metal-working industrial enterprises of Donbas.

11   Vladimir Kornilov, «*Донецко-Криворожская республика. Расстрелянная мечта*» (2017), ISBN 978-5-496-03067-0.

12   Abibok, 'On the way to creating the 'Donbas people' – Identity policy in the self-proclaimed republics in east Ukraine', p.5.

13   Charles Clover, *Black Wind, White Snow – The rise of Russia's new nationalism* (New Haven: Yale 2016), p.12.

14   Clover, *Black Wind, White Snow – The rise of Russia's new nationalism*, p.2.

15   Swain, *Re-constructing the Post-Soviet Industrial Region: The Donbas in transition*.

16   Swain, *Re-constructing the Post-Soviet Industrial Region: The Donbas in transition*.

17   Anna Matveeva, 'No Moscow stooges: identity polarization and guerrilla movements in Donbass', *Southeast European and Black Sea Studies*, 16:1 (2016), pp.25–50, DOI:10.1080/14683857.2016.1148415, p.37.

18   Anon, 'Peace in Ukraine (III): The Costs of War in Donbas', *International Crisis Group*, Report No. 261 (3 Sept 2020), https://www.crisisgroup.org/europe-central-asia/eastern-europe/ukraine/261-peace-ukraine-iii-costs-war-donbas

19   Pål Kolstø, 'Crimea vs. Donbas: How Putin Won Russian Nationalist Support—and Lost it Again', *Slavic Review* 75, no. 3 (Fall 2016), p.714.

20   Anon, 'Peace in Ukraine (III): The Costs of War in Donbas'.

21   «Требуются наводчики, зарплата достойная». Сколько платят наемникам «ЛДНР», *Krim Realii* website, 1 July 2019, https://ru.krymr.com/a/skolko-platyat-naemnikam-ldnr/30031770.html

22   Taras Kuzio, *Putin's War Against Ukraine – Revolution, Nationalism, and Crime* (CreateSpace Independent Publishing Platform, 2017), ISBN 978-1543285864, p.21.

23   Quoted in Malyarenko and Galbreath, 'Paramilitary Motivation in Ukraine', p.129.

24   Matveeva, *Through Times of Trouble – Conflict in Southeastern Ukraine Explained from Within*, p.115.

Chapter 3

1   Joshua Yaffa, *Between Two Fires – Truth, ambition and compromise in Putin's Russia* (London: Granta, 2020)(uncorrected bound proof, Jan 2020), p.227.

2   Sergei Medvedev, *The Return of the Russian Leviathan* (Cambridge: Polity, 2020), p.202.

3   Vicky Davis, *Myth Making in the Soviet Union and Modern Russia – Remembering World War II in Brezhnev's Hero City* (London: Bloomsbury 2020), p.228.

4   Clover, *Black Wind, White Snow – The rise of Russia's new nationalism*, p.13.

5   Maxim Edwards, 'Symbolism of the Donetsk People's Republic', *Open Democracy* website, 9 June 2014, https://www.opendemocracy.net/en/odr/symbolism-of-donetsk-peoples-republic-flag-novorossiya/

6   Kolstø, 'Symbol of the War — But Which One? The St George Ribbon in Russian Nation-Building'.

7   Daisy Sindelar, 'What's Orange And Black And Bugging Ukraine?', *Radio Free Europe* website, 28 April 2014, https://www.rferl.org/a/ukraine-colorado-beetle-separatists/25365793.html

8   Artem Shevchenko, *Slovyansk: The Beginning of the War* (Folio, 2020), ISBN 978-9660394155; p.45.

9   Kolstø, 'Symbol of the War — But Which One? The St George Ribbon in Russian Nation-Building', p.700.

Chapter 4

1   Дмитрий Дурнев, 'Карта акторов конфликта на Донбассе: локальные акторы ОРДО' (CivilM+ 2020), p.35. The original text reads: 'Продвигает идею замирения с Украиной в виде выстраивания «бетонной стены» на линии пересечения на 20 лет и только потом, после охлаждения взаимной ненависти, по его мнению, надо начинать переговоры «по типу Приднестровских»'

2   Matveeva, *Through Times of Trouble – Conflict in Southeastern Ukraine Explained from Within*, p.100.

3   Paweł Pieniążek, *Greetings from Novorossiya: Eyewitness to the War in Ukraine* (Pittsburgh: University of Pittsburgh Press, 2017), p.90.

4   The name itself literally means 'Little Russia' and was a term sometimes used in the Russian Empire to describe the area now forming modern-day Ukraine.

5   Kathrin Hille and Roman Olearchyk, 'Call for new Ukraine state serves Moscow's goals', *Financial Times*, 22 Jul 2017.

6   de Waal and von Twickel, *Beyond Frozen Conflict – Scenarios for the separatist disputes of Eastern Europe*, p.106.

7   Yaffa, *Between Two Fires – Truth, ambition and compromise in Putin's Russia*, p.275.

8   Bettina Renz and Hanna Smith, *Russia and hybrid warfare: Going beyond the label* (Helsinki: Kikimora Publications at the Aleksanteri Institute, University of Helsinki, Finland, 2016), p.14.

9   Tony Wood, *Russia Without Putin: Money, Power and the Myths of the New Cold War* (London: Verso, 2018), p.133.

10   Igor Sutyagin and Justin Bronk, *Russia's New Ground Forces: Capabilities, Limitations and Implications for International Security* (Abingdon: Routledge, 2017), p.105.

Chapter 5

1   Toal, *Near Abroad – Putin, the West, and the contest over Ukraine and the Caucasus*, p.77.

2   Richard Sakwa, *Frontline Ukraine – Crisis in the borderlands* (London: I B Tauris, 2014), p.151.

3   Pieniążek, *Greetings from Novorossiya: Eyewitness to the War in Ukraine*, p.20.

4   Matveeva, *Through Times of Trouble – Conflict in Southeastern Ukraine Explained from Within*, p.106.

5   Shevchenko, *Slovyansk: The Beginning of the War*, p.210.

6   Matveeva, *Through Times of Trouble – Conflict in Southeastern Ukraine Explained from Within*, p.107.

7   Simon Shuster, 'Exclusive: Meet the Pro-Russian Separatists of Eastern Ukraine', 23 April 2014, *Time* Magazine, https://time.com/74405/exclusive-pro-russian-separatists-eastern-ukraine/

8   Pieniążek, *Greetings from Novorossiya: Eyewitness to the War in Ukraine*, p.73.

9   'В Славянске террористы "Стрелкова" замордовали протестантского пастора и его детей', iPress UA website, 21 July 2014, https://ipress.ua/ru/news/v_slavyanske_terrorysti_strelkova_zamordovaly_protestantskogo_pastora_y_ego_detey_75748.html

10   This depot, located in an old salt mine, is described in detail in Christopher J. Chivers, *The Gun: The Story of the AK-47* (London: Penguin 2011).

11   Shevchenko, *Slovyansk: The Beginning of the War*, p.255.

12   Yekelchyk, *The Conflict in Ukraine*, p.147.

13   Paul Goble, 'Why People in Eastern Ukraine Haven't Flocked to Secessionist Banners', *The Interpreter* website, 29 Jul 2014, https://www.interpretermag.com/why-people-in-eastern-ukraine-havent-flocked-to-secessionist-banners/

14   Shevchenko, *Slovyansk: The Beginning of the War*, p.304.

15   Jim Roberts, 'Ukraine Government Claims Control of Airport; Up to 50 Separatists Are Killed', *Mashable* website, 27 May 2014, https://mashable.com/archive/at-least-30-dead-in-ukraine-airport-battle

16   In English, the word translates literally as 'military supply/surplus shop'. The name referred to a comment made by Russian President Vladimir Putin in 2014 with reference to the 'Polite People' who seized Crimea, in which he claimed that they were all local volunteers who had bought their weapons, uniforms and equipment in military surplus shops. This was before his later acknowledgement that Russian military forces had been involved in the operation.

17   Matveeva, *Through Times of Trouble – Conflict in Southeastern Ukraine Explained from Within*, pp.150–151.

18   Anon, Ukraine crisis: Rebel military chief Strelkov 'quits', BBC News website, 14 August 2014, https://www.bbc.com/news/world-europe-28792966

19   Clover, *Black Wind, White Snow – The rise of Russia's new nationalism*, p.327.

20   Michael Kofman, Katya Migacheva, Brian Nichiporuk, Andrew Radin, Olesya Tkacheva and Jenny Oberholtzer, *Lessons from Russia's Operations in Crimea and Eastern Ukraine* (Santa Monica: RAND Corporation, 2017), pp.56–57.

21   The Ukrainian perspective of this street fighting was dramatised in the 2019 Ukrainian film *Ilovaisk 2014: Donbas Battalion*, directed by Ivan Tymchenko. For further information on the film refer to: https://www.imdb.com/title/tt10276554/

22   Amos C. Fox, 'The Siege Of Ilovaisk: Manufactured Insurgencies And Decision In War', Association of the United States Army website, 23 April 2021, https://www.ausa.org/publications/siege-ilovaisk-manufactured-insurgencies-and-decision-war

23   Aric Toler, 'How These Adorable Puppies Exposed Russian Involvement in Ukraine', Bellingcat website, 11 March 2015, https://www.bellingcat.com/news/uk-and-europe/2015/03/11/vreditel-sobaka/

24   The Russian language name for the Ukrainian city of Horlivka, indicating the direction from which the strike group would be attacking.

25   Randy Noorman, 'The Battle of Debaltseve: a Hybrid Army in a Classic Battle of Encirclement', *Small Wars Journal*, 17 July 2020, https://smallwarsjournal.com/jrnl/art/battle-debaltseve-hybrid-army-classic-battle-encirclement

26   Anon, '#MinskMonitor: Wagner's Role in Key Ukrainian Battle Revealed', DFRLab website, 12 July 2018, https://medium.com/dfrlab/minskmonitor-wagners-role-in-key-ukrainian-battle-revealed-95ee8ce133fe

27   Noorman, 'The Battle of Debaltseve: a Hybrid Army in a Classic Battle of Encirclement'.

28   Stefan Huijboom, 'Quieter, but guns of war still not silent, on first day of cease-fire in Donetsk', Kyiv Post, 15 Feb 2015.

29   Anon, '"Зона беспощадной торговли": боевики "ДНР" открыли "дьюти-фри" на границе с Украиной', RBK Ukraine website, 22 October 2016, https://styler.rbc.ua/rus/zhizn/zona-besposhchadnoy-torgovli-boeviki-dnr-1477153887.html

30   Anon, 'Oligarch Akmetov's plants in occupied Donbas stop production amid trade blockade', Euromaidan Press website, 22 February 2017, https://euromaidanpress.com/2017/02/22/akhmetovs-companies-halt-production-due-to-blockade/

31   de Waal and von Twickel, Beyond Frozen Conflict – Scenarios for the separatist disputes of Eastern Europe, p.34.

32   Lawrence Freedman, Ukraine and the Art of Strategy (Oxford: Oxford University Press, 2019), pp.117–118.

33   Mark Voyger, 'The potential winter unfreezing of the Donbas', The Ukrainian Week, February 2020, #2 (144), p.34.

34   Anon, 'Pikuzy residents demand that Russian mercenaries leave village', UNIAN website, 3 October 2017, https://www.unian.info/war/2167289-pikuzy-residents-demand-that-russian-mercenaries-leave-village.html

35   Anon, 'В ДНР упраздняют министерство обороны Об этом сообщает "Рамблер"', Rambler website, 9 September 2018, https://news.rambler.ru/world/40758729-v-dnr-uprazdnyayut-ministerstvo-oborony/

Chapter 6

1   Medvedev, The Return of the Russian Leviathan, p.25.

2   Anon, 'How Russia controls occupied Donbas', Ukrinform website, 1 February 2021, https://www.ukrinform.net/rubric-polytics/3182285-how-russia-controls-occupied-donbas.html

3   Sutyagin and Bronk, Russia's New Ground Forces: Capabilities, Limitations and Implications for International Security, p.111.

4   Anon, 'Joint Forces Commander: Over 2,000 Russian career officers stationed in occupied Donbas', Ukraine Ministry of Defence website, 30 April 2020, https://www.mil.gov.ua/en/news/2020/04/30/joint-forces-commander-over-2-000-russian-career-officers-stationed-in-occupied-donbas/

5   As an example: Andrzej Wilk, 'Eyes west! A shift in focus in Russia's Southern Military District', Centre for Eastern Studies website, 8 September 2020, https://www.osw.waw.pl/en/publikacje/osw-commentary/2020-09-08/eyes-west-a-shift-focus-russias-southern-military-district

6   Anon, 'Direct dialogue with "L/DPR", COVID-19 and more – Weekly Update on Ukraine #10, 09 – 15 March', Ukraine Crisis Media Centre website, 16 March 2020, https://uacrisis.org/en/75240-weekly-update-ukraine-10-09-15-march

7   Matveeva, Through Times of Trouble – Conflict in Southeastern Ukraine Explained from Within, p.134.

8   Andrei Kolesnikov, 'Why the Kremlin Is Shutting Down the Novorossiya Project', Carnegie Endowment for International Peace website, 29 May 2015, https://carnegiemoscow.org/commentary/60249

9   Duncan Allan, The Minsk Conundrum: Western Policy and Russia's War in Eastern Ukraine (London: Chatham House 2020), accessed via https://www.chathamhouse.org/2020/05/minsk-conundrum-western-policy-and-russias-war-eastern-ukraine-0/background-minsk

10   Anon, 'Intelligence data on 1st and 2nd Army Corps of Russian Federation in occupied Donbas', InformNapalm website, 8 September 2020, https://informnapalm.org/en/intelligence-data-on-1st-and-2nd-army-corps-of-russian-federation-in-occupied-donbas/

11   Freedman, Ukraine and the Art of Strategy, pp.158–159.

Chapter 7

1   Anon, '«Армейские корпуса» реорганизовали в «оперативно-тактические объединения», обновлён командный состав – данные исследования «СтопТеррор»', Ukraine Crisis Media Centre website, 11 August 2018, https://uacrisis.org/ru/45994-kabakaev

2   Сергій Горбатенко, 'Может ли 1-й российский армейский корпус стать народной милицией в Украине?', Radio Svoboda website, 16 December 2020, https://www.radiosvoboda.org/a/31004129.html

3   Michael J Sheldon, 'An anniversary assessment of the armed forces of the Donetsk Peoples Republic', Afghan Hindsight Wordpress, 29 January 2016, https://afghanhindsight.wordpress.com/2016/01/29/an-anniversary-assessment-of-the-armed-forces-of-the-donetsk-peoples-republic/

4   Anon, '70% бойовиків на Донбасі – громадяни Росії, 25% – кадрові військові та 45% – так звані «добровольці», – воєнна розвідка', Ukraine Crisis Media Centre website, 17 April 2016, https://uacrisis.org/uk/42505-voyenna-rozvidka-2

5   Anon, 'Intelligence data on 1st and 2nd Army Corps of Russian Federation in occupied Donbas', InformNapalm website, 8 September 2020, https://informnapalm.org/en/intelligence-data-on-1st-and-2nd-army-corps-of-russian-federation-in-occupied-donbas/

6   'Sword' in Russian (меч).

7   A Soviet or Russian 'divizion' (Russian: дивизион) is a unit of artillery equivalent to a battalion, not to be confused with the much larger 'division' in English (Russian: дивизия).

8   Anon, '1-я Отдельная Славянская Мотострелковая Бригада (1 ОСМБР)', StopTerror website, 1 October 2015, https://stopterror.in.ua/info/2015/10/1-ya-otdelnaya-Slavyansk-motostrelkovaya-brigada-1-osmbr-v-ch-08801/

9   Anon, '1 Отдельная "Славянская" Мотострелковая Бригада', Oneparatrooper Live Journal, 9 Feb 2016, https://oneparatrooper.livejournal.com/2145.html

10   i.e. the city of Kostiantynivka in Donetsk oblast.

11   'Их подвиг бессмертен. Константиновский разведбат'; YouTube website; 10 May 2021; https://www.youtube.com/watch?v=XwZp5pNz57Y

12   Sakwa, Frontline Ukraine – Crisis in the borderlands, p.170.

13   Julia Ioffe, 'I Met Igor Bezler, the Russian Rebel Who Said, "We Have Just Shot Down a Plane"', The New Republic website, 18 July 2014, https://newrepublic.com/article/118770/who-igor-bezler-russian-rebel-implicated-malaysia-flight-17

14   Anon, 'Торловские бесы – по следам 3й ОМСБр "Беркут"', Oneparatrooper Live Journal website 2016, https://oneparatrooper.livejournal.com/13616.html

15   Anon, '3rd Separate Motorized Rifle Brigade "Berkut" (3 OMBr)', Stop Terror website, 3 October 2015, https://stopterror.in.ua/info/2015/10/3-ya-otdelnaya-motostrelkovaya-brigada-berkut-3-ombr-v-ch-08803/

16   'Дивизион "Корсы". Готовность № 1', YouTube, 30 July 2018, https://www.youtube.com/watch?v=yUzXMbhsWo0

17   Мустафа Найем, 'Лидер харьковского "Оплота" Евгений Жилин: Мне не нравится, что давят на моего президента', Ukrainskaya Pravda website, 6 February 2014, https://www.pravda.com.ua/rus/articles/2014/02/6/7012996/

18   Tim Judah, In Wartime: Stories from Ukraine (London: Penguin, 2016), p.179.

19   Anon, 'Оплота захватили здание Донецкого горсовета', Novaya Gazeta Ru website, 16 April 2014, https://novayagazeta.ru/news/2014/04/16/99454-boytsy-harkovskogo-171-oplota-187-zahvatili-zdanie-donetskogo-gorsoveta

20 Anon, 'Глава "Оплота" Евгений Жилин убит при покушении в ресторане под Москвой', Life Ru website, 2016, https://life.ru/p/905585

21 A first sign of this transfer was observed by open-source researchers focused on the unit patches of DPR armed formation units, an interesting use of open-source research in observing the DPR. See: 'Подразделения ополчения НОВОРОССИИ: в шевронах, нашивках, знамёнах и знаках отличия. (upd 2/09/14)', ce48 Live Journal website, 5 August 2014, https://ce48.livejournal.com/1891.html

22 Телеканал Оплот ТВ, https://www.youtube.com/channel/UC9ZreNsl6acYx22Y0Tt-JzQ

23 Anon, '5-я Отдельная Мотострелковая Бригада «Оплот» (5 ОМБР)', Stop Terror website, 5 October 2015, https://stopterror.in.ua/info/2015/10/5-ya-otdelnaya-motostrelkovaya-brigada-oplot-5-ombr-v-ch-08805/

24 В'ячеслав Хрипун, 'Какие группировки воюют на Донбассе с украинской армией и между собой', The Insider website, 22 October 2014, http://www.theinsider.ua/politics/544551695677e/

25 'РЕСПУБЛИКАНСКАЯ ГВАРДИЯ ДНР (Сборник фотофактов)', ce48 Live Journal, 21 July 2015, https://ce48.livejournal.com/5733.html

26 Michael J Sheldon, 'Clipped wings – on the "DPR" Republican Guard and reforms in the separatist militia', afghanhindsight Wordpress, 25 October 2016, https://afghanhindsight.wordpress.com/2016/10/25/clipped-wings-on-the-dpr-republican-guard-and-reforms-in-the-separatist-militia/

27 'Путь правды. Главнокомандующий Республиканской Гвардии', YouTube, 16 June 2015, https://www.youtube.com/watch?v=P-1EE7nnktQ

28 Anon, 'Республиканская Гвардия ДНР', Stop Terror website, November 2015, https://stopterror.in.ua/info/2015/11/respublikanskaya-gvardiya-dnr/

29 Anon, '"Трактористы и шахтеры": кто воюет в Донбассе в составе батальона "Пятнашка"', Dialog UA website, 16 February 2016, https://www.dialog.ua/news/78762_1455621232

30 Олег Панфилов, '"Пятнашка". Кто воюет за боевиков на Донбассе', NV Ukraine website, 11 January 2018, https://nv.ua/opinion/pjatnashka-kto-vojuet-za-boevikov-na-donbasse-2444486.html

31 Дмитро Путята, 'Хто воює проти нас 9 ТА 11 ОМСП сепаратистів', Tyzhden Ukraine website, 14 November 2019, https://tyzhden.ua/Society/237694

32 Anon, 'Морпехи мелкого моря', Oneparatrooper Live Journal, 2 July 2016, https://oneparatrooper.livejournal.com/17346.html

33 Anon, 'Боевая подготовка морской пехоты ДНР', BMPD Live Journal, 23 August 2016, https://bmpd.livejournal.com/2082023.html

34 Александр Широкорад, 'Кто в Азовском море хозяин?', Zvezda Weekly website, 11 April 2018, https://zvezdaweekly.ru/news/2018491241-DJmWG.html

35 Anon, '9th Separate Motorized Rifle Regiment of the DPR of the 1st AK NO MO DPR', Stop Terror website, 9 October 2015, https://stopterror.in.ua/info/2015/10/9-j-otdelnyj-motostrelkovyj-polk-dnr-1-go-ak-no-mo-dnr-v-ch-08819/

36 Дмитро Путята, 'Хто воює проти нас 9 ТА 11 ОМСП сепаратистів', Tyzhden Ukraine website, 14 November 2019, https://tyzhden.ua/Society/237694

37 Anon, '11 отдельный Енакиевско-Дунайский мотострелковый полк «Восток»', Stop Terror website, 11 October 2015, https://stopterror.in.ua/info/2015/10/11-otdelnyj-enakievsko-dunajskij-motostrelkovyj-polk-v-ch-08818-vostok/

38 Claire Bigg, 'Vostok Battalion, A Powerful New Player In Eastern Ukraine', Radio Free Europe website, 30 May 2014, https://www.rferl.org/a/vostok-battalion-a-powerful-new-player-in-eastern-ukraine/25404785.html

39 Катерина Сергацкова, 'У таборі батальйону "Схід"', Pravda Ukraine website, 2 June 2014, https://www.pravda.com.ua/articles/2014/06/2/7027718/

40 Mairbek Vatchagaev, 'Understanding the Mysterious Appearance of the Chechen 'Vostok' Battalion in Eastern Ukraine', Jamestown Foundation website, 30 May 2014, https://jamestown.org/program/understanding-the-mysterious-appearance-of-the-chechen-vostok-battalion-in-eastern-ukraine-2/

41 'Donetsk Live №66 Ходаковский Александр Ответы на все вопросы', YouTube, 18 October 2015, https://www.youtube.com/watch?v=pCeoagzwvoc&t=273s

42 Anon, 'По ситуации с "Востоком"', Colonelcassad Live Journal, 8 October 2015, https://colonelcassad.livejournal.com/2420753.html

43 'Тест-драйв отжатой у ВСУ (Новой) БТР-4'; YouTube; 12 October 2014; https://www.youtube.com/watch?v=WVzCQ4EFMVA

44 Anon, 'ХОДАКОВСКИЙ: БРИГАДА «ВОСТОК» ПОТЕРЯЛА БОЛЬШЕ 500 ЧЕЛОВЕК', Novosti Donbassa website, 10 July 2017, https://novosti.dn.ua/news/272130-khodakovskyy-brygada-vostok-poteryala-bolshe-500-chelovek

45 Anon, 'Бригада (батальон) "Восток" и ее трансформации', Ru_chevron Live Journal, 15 August 2016, https://ru-chevron.livejournal.com/93227.html

46 The Russian spelling of Makiivka, a large city to the immediate east of Donetsk.

47 Anon, 'Командир полка спецназа ДНР Евгений РЯДНОВ: У меня восемь детей, и в 2014-м надо было выбирать, в какой стране они жить будут', Donetsk Komsomolskaya Pravda website, 31 March 2018, https://www.donetsk.kp.ru/daily/26813.5/3849256/

48 Anon, 'Полк специального назначения Министерства обороны ДНР', Ronin_077 LiveJournal, 2 April 2019, https://ronin-077.livejournal.com/82489.html

49 Yuri Zoria, 'Coup attempt underway in occupied Luhansk: what we know so far', Euromaidan Press website, 22 November 2017, https://euromaidanpress.com/2017/11/22/coup-attempt-in-occupied-luhansk-what-we-know-so-far/

50 Anon, 'Батальон Прилепина', 11 October 2017, https://nstarikov.ru/batalon-prilepina-85403

51 Anon, '#MinskMonitor: The Rise and Fall of "Prilepin's Battalion"', DFR Lab, 8 November 2018, https://medium.com/dfrlab/minskmonitor-the-rise-and-fall-of-prilepins-battalion-f9655393df48

52 Anon, 'Отдельный разведывательный батальон Морской пехоты «Спарта»', Stop Terror website, November 2015, https://stopterror.in.ua/info/2015/11/otdelnyj-razvedyvatelnyj-batalon-morskoj-pehoty-sparta-v-ch-08806/

53 Donbass; a 2018 film directed by Sergei Loznitsa.

54 Anon, 'New evidence of summary killings of Ukrainian soldiers must spark urgent investigations', 9 April 2015, Amnesty International website, https://www.amnesty.org/en/latest/news/2015/04/ukraine-new-evidence-of-summary-killings-of-captured-soldiers-must-spark-urgent-investigations/

55 Shaun Walker, 'Prominent rebel warlord Arseny 'Motorola' Pavlov dies in Donetsk blast', The Guardian website, 17 October 2016.

56 The film His Battalion («Его батальон») can be found in numerous places online, e.g. at YouTube: 'Документальный фильм News Front «Его батальон» — фильм Максима Фадеева памяти «Моторолы»', YouTube, 29 May 2020, https://www.youtube.com/watch?v=dw0p9-bldok

57 Anon, 'Батальон "Спарта" – спецназ ДНР', Soldati RU website, 7 Jan 2021, https://www.soldati-russian.ru/publ/bratskaja_novorossija_donbass/materialy_o_vojne_v_novorossii/batalon_sparta_specnaz_dnr/

58 Зайцев Василий, 'Боевики "воруют" эмблемы для своих банд из компьютерных игр', Segodnya Ukraine website, 25 November

2014, https://www.segodnya.ua/regions/donetsk/boeviki-voruyut-emblemy-dlya-svoih-band-iz-kompyuternyh-igr-572052.html

59 '"Гиви" под обстрелом рсзо "Град" / Givi and MLRS "Grad" shell strike. 05.10.2014', YouTube, 14 October 2014, https://www.youtube.com/watch?v=Aq6axh5x_l4

60 Matveeva, 'No Moscow stooges: identity polarization and guerrilla movements in Donbass', pp.33–34.

61 Anon, 'ТАНКОВЫЕ БАТАЛЬОНЫ ДНР, номера машин в фотофакта', ce48 Live Journal, 19 April 2015, https://ce48.livejournal.com/3835.html

62 'Соревнования танковых экипажей ВС ДНР 2017', YouTube, 5 September 2017, https://www.youtube.com/watch?v=LPviPHOlNyw

63 "Lost' T-72B Tank from Ulan-Ude Was Found in Ukraine', InformNapalm website, 21 March 2016, https://informnapalm.org/en/mar20-lost-t-72b/

64 'Танковый биатлон между экипажами ДНР 31 08 2017, 'Панорама', YouTube, 2 September 2017, https://www.youtube.com/watch?v=DaG3EO7SpmU

65 Александра Полищук, 'В "ДНР" задержали известного комбата боевиков "Дизеля", который воевал в ДАП и Дебальцево', Depo Donbass website, 5 October 2021, https://dn.depo.ua/rus/donetsk/u-dnr-zatrimali-vidomogo-kombata-boyovikiv-dizelya-yakiy-voyuvav-v-dap-ta-debaltsevomu-202110051376087

66 'Боевые учения батальона «Хан». Часть 1. ТВ СВ-ДНР Выпуск 500', YouTube website, 4 July 2015, https://youtu.be/Xsu9pcN2hgI

67 Anon, 'В батальоне «Хан»', EOT-DNR Live Journal, 9 August 2016, https://eot-dnr.livejournal.com/233422.html

68 Anon, 'Подразделения ополчения НОВОРОССИИ: в шевронах, нашивках, знамёнах и знаках отличия 2 (upd 14/04/15)', ce48 Live Journal, 24 October 2014, https://ce48.livejournal.com/2214.html

69 Anon, 'ДонВОКУ: фабрика по производству офицеров', Vse DNR website, 17 May 2015, https://vsednr.ru/donvoku-fabrika-po-proizvodstvu-oficerov/

70 Anon, 'Освобождение Мариуполя: морпехи Новороссии против морпехов Украинского Государства', 9111 Ru website, 24 March 2022, https://www.9111.ru/questions/7777777771798268/

71 The population of ethnic Greeks living in the southern part of Donetsk oblast and other places along the Black Sea coast in Ukraine trace their settlements to the eighteenth century, when they were encouraged to move there by the Russian Empire from Crimea, then under Ottoman control.

Chapter 8

1 Anon, 'Донбасс сравнялся с Киевом по военной мощи', MKRU website, 23 July 2018, https://www.mk.ru/politics/2018/07/23/donbass-sravnyalsya-s-kievom-po-voennoy-moshhi.html

2 Anon, 'В ДНР появятся внутренние войска МВД', Interfax website, 20 March 2015, https://www.interfax.ru/world/431265

3 'Подготовка бронетехники Отряда "Легион"', YouTube, 5 April 2018, https://www.youtube.com/watch?v=2gCikUgLNcA

4 Александр Исак, 'Донбасс после Захарченко. Окончательный поворот в пользу России', Radio Svoboda website, 16 September 2018, https://www.svoboda.org/a/29492550.html

5 Anon, 'Подразделение спецназначения "Витязь" Министерства транспорта ДНР', Ronin_077 Live Journal, 24 February 2016, https://ronin-077.livejournal.com/31229.html

Chapter 9

1 Verbatim Record in the case concerning Application of the International Convention for the Suppression of the Financing of Terrorism and of the International Convention on the Elimination of All Forms of Racial Discrimination (Ukraine v. Russian Federation), 7 March 2017, International Court of Justice The Hague, pp.20–21.

2 Jonathan Ferguson and N. R. Jenzen-Jones, *Raising Red Flags: An Examination of Arms and Munitions in the Ongoing Conflict in Ukraine* (ARES, 2014), p.87.

3 Anon, '«Новороссия» сливает Россию: «чемодан радистки Кэт», российские «Печенеги» и «Корды», InformNapalm website, 15 May 2015, https://informnapalm.org/9291-novorossyya-slyvaet-rossyyu-chemodan-radystky-ket-y-rossyjskye-pechenegy-s-kordom/

4 'Трофейный российский ПКП "Печенег" у ВСУ', YouTube, 16 June 2015, https://www.youtube.com/watch?v=lPO3-4AIyIk

5 Vera Zimmerman, 'The Role of Snipers in the Donbas Trench War', Eurasia Daily Monitor Volume 17 Issue 26, 25 Feb 2020, https://jamestown.org/program/the-role-of-snipers-in-the-donbas-trench-war/

6 Руслан Рудомский, 'Запрещенные противопехотные мины на Донбассе: Что за оружие придумали боевики "Л-ДНР"', Depo UA website, 20 October 2020, https://www.depo.ua/rus/war/zaboroneni-protipikhotni-mini-na-donbasi-shcho-za-zbroyu-pridumali-boyoviki-l-dnr-202010201231664

7 'Это Донбасс мина 82- мм на РПГ 7;)', YouTube, 17 April 2016, https://www.youtube.com/watch?v=F52YDcXNlDo

8 Anon, 'Не можна виявити металошукачами: нові поставки мін росіянами на Донбас', Militarny website, 9 July 2018, https://mil.in.ua/uk/ne-mozhna-vyyavyty-metaloshukachamy-novi-postavky-min-rosiyanamy-na-donbas/

9 'Ukraine's request for an extension of the deadline for completing the destruction of Anti-personnel Mines in accordance with Article 5 of the Ottawa Convention', AP Mine Ban Convention website, 26 November 2020, https://www.apminebanconvention.org/fileadmin/APMBC/MSP/18MSP/statements/8-Ukraine-full.pdf

10 James Miller, Pierre Vaux, Catherine A. Fitzpatrick, and Michael Weiss, *An Invasion by Any Other Name: The Kremlin's Dirty War in Ukraine* (New York: Frontline Printing, 2015), p.15.

11 Anon, 'The Battle of Ilovaisk', Forensic Architecture website, 19 Aug 2019, https://forensic-architecture.org/investigation/the-battle-of-ilovaisk

12 Veli-Pekka Kivimäki, 'Tankspotting: T-90As in the Donbass', Bellingcat website, 2 April 2017, https://www.bellingcat.com/news/uk-and-europe/2017/04/02/tankspotting-t-90as-donbass/

13 'Tank Chats #54 JS III | The Tank Museum', YouTube, 28 July 2018, https://www.youtube.com/watch?v=EdkJlTSIMYU

14 Anon, 'Танк ИС-3 в войне на Донбассе – Полная история', Militarny website, 20 October 2019, https://mil.in.ua/uk/blogs/tank-ys-3-v-vojne-na-donbasse-polnaya-ystoryya/

15 Anon, 'Russian proxy "DNR" displays modernised BMP-2 with Kontakt-1 ERA in Ukraine's occupied Donetsk region', Live UA map website, 16 April 2018, https://liveuamap.com/en/2018/16-april-russian-proxy-dnr-displays-modernised-bmp2-with

16 Anon, 'Модернизированный БТР-80 на вооружении российских оккупационных войск на Донбассе', InformNapalm website, 18 October 2016, https://informnapalm.org/28672-modernizirovannyj-btr-80/

17 Anon, 'OSCE spots 15 newest Russian UAZ Esaul armored vehicles in Donbas (Drone photo)', InformNapalm website, 3 May 2021, https://informnapalm.org/en/osce-spots-15-newest-russian-uaz-esaul-armored-vehicles-in-donbas-drone-photo/

18 Sutyagin and Bronk, *Russia's New Ground Forces: Capabilities, Limitations and Implications for International Security*, p.58.

19 Soviet and Russian self-propelled tube artillery systems were generally named after flowers; Gvozdika (carnation); Akatsia (acacia); and Giatsint (hyacinth).

20 Anon, 'Тремящий "Кальмиус"', OneParatrooper Live Journal, 9 October 2016, https://oneparatrooper.livejournal.com/19600.html

21 Anon, 'New Russian 2B26 Grad launch rocket system in Donbas', InformNapalm website, 12 July 2020, https://informnapalm.org/en/new-russian-2b26-grad-launch-rocket-system-in-donbas/

22 Soviet and Russian rocket artillery systems are generally named after violent weather events; Grad (hail); Uragan (hurricane); and Smerch (tornado or whirlwind).

23 Galeotti makes this claim in *Armies of Russia's War in Ukraine*, p.27. Matveeva similarly claims that the DPR/LPR acquired the earlier TOS-1 Buratino MLRS in *Through Times of Trouble – Conflict in Southeastern Ukraine Explained from Within*, p.151 but the claim is not referenced. It is worth noting that the one reported sighting of the TOS-1 by the international observer mission has never been triangulated with any other sources.

24 Anon, 'Information on the use of Russian heavy flamethrower systems in Donbas', InformNapalm website, 2 November 2021, https://informnapalm.org/en/information-on-the-use-of-russian-heavy-flamethrower-systems-in-donbas

25 Anon, 'Ракетные войска сепаратистов: правда и вымысел', Bellingcat website, 23 June 2018, https://ru.bellingcat.com/novosti/ukraine/2018/06/23/dnr-rocket-forces/

26 '28.05.2017. Наслідки обстрілу населеного пункту Красногорівка терористами ДНР', YouTube, 28 May 2017, https://www.youtube.com/watch?v=E2WvG27-i2A. The distinctive tail section of the 'Chinese' can be seen at approximately 1:52 in the video.

27 'Awesome Low Pass of Ukrainian Mig-29, over Slovyansk (Ukraine Crisis)', YouTube, 16 April 2014; https://www.youtube.com/watch?v=ZokhRnJ3-EQ

28 Miller, Vaux, Fitzpatrick, and Weiss, *An Invasion by Any Other Name: The Kremlin's Dirty War in Ukraine*, p.17.

29 Case Concerning Application Of The International Convention For The Suppression Of The Financing Of Terrorism And Of The International Convention On The Elimination Of All Forms Of Racial Discrimination (Ukraine V. Russian Federation), International Court of Justice, 12 June 2018; p.81.

30 Sutyagin and Bronk, *Russia's New Ground Forces: Capabilities, Limitations and Implications for International Security*, p.115. Note: The original quote references the 'Strela-10 (SA-9)', but the NATO reporting name of the 9K35 Strela-10 used by the DPR armed formations is in fact (in NATO reporting terms) the SA-13 Gopher, on an MT-LB chassis.

31 Anon, '#MinskMonitor: OSCE Drone Takes Fire Amid Continued Escalation of Hostilities', DFRLab website, 5 July 2018, https://medium.com/dfrlab/minskmonitor-osce-drone-takes-fire-amid-continued-escalation-of-hostilities-994c4cb5a18c

32 Anon, 'Russian radars detected in eastern Ukraine', DFR Lab website, 11 March 2021, https://medium.com/dfrlab/russian-radars-detected-in-eastern-ukraine-fb625ec4de16

33 The criminal investigation by the Joint Investigation Team (JIT), Netherlands Prosecution Service website, undated, https://www.prosecutionservice.nl/topics/mh17-plane-crash/criminal-investigation-jit-mh17

34 Anon, 'Ukraine's pro-Russian rebels reject Dutch MH17 report', BBC News website, 14 October 2015, https://www.bbc.com/news/world-europe-34530906

35 Anton Zverev, 'Exclusive: Ukraine rebel commander acknowledges fighters had BUK missile', Reuters website, 23 July 2014, https://www.reuters.com/article/us-ukraine-crisis-commander-exclusive-idUSKBN0FS1V920140723

36 Ukrainian Ministry of Defence Twitter post, 26 October 2021, https://twitter.com/DefenceU/status/1453073184442523650

37 Matveeva, *Through Times of Trouble – Conflict in Southeastern Ukraine Explained from Within*, p.128.

38 Anon, 'Авиация Новороссии – 1-я ОАЭ БПЛА «Гренада»', Linur2 Live Journal, 8 August 2014, https://linur2.livejournal.com/842315.html

39 Anon, 'Deadly DIY Drones In The Donbas', RFE/RL website, 21 Feb 2020, https://www.rferl.org/a/deadly-diy-drones-in-the-donbas/30445714.html

40 'Боевики «ДНР» попытались заминировать минами ПОМ-2 дорожный коридор «Горловка-Бахмут»', Novosti Donbassa website, 15 April 2021, https://news.dn.ua/news/11407boeviki-dnr-popytalis-zaminirovat-minami-pom-2-dorozhnyi-koridor-gorlovka-bahmut.html

41 Anon, 'Росія на Донбасі використовує більше 8 типів БПЛА', InformNapalm website, 22 March 2019, https://informnapalm.org/ua/rosiia-na-donbasi-vykorystovuie-bilshe-8/

42 'Оружие России на Донбассе: что уже там – и что поставят еще?', Radio Svoboda website, 31 January 2022, https://www.radiosvoboda.org/a/rossijskoe-oruzhije-donbass/31675850.html

43 Anon, 'Russian command sends army drone systems to Donbas – photo evidence', InformNapalm website, 19 April 2017, https://informnapalm.org/en/russian-command-sends-army-drone-systems-donbas-photo-evidence/

44 Anon, 'Российские системы РЭБ на Донбассе стали чаще попадать на фото. Эксклюзивные данные', InformNapalm website, 13 March 2020, https://informnapalm.org/48525-rossijskie-sistemy-reb-na-donbasse/

45 Anon, Weapons of the War in Ukraine: A three-year investigation of weapon supplies into Donetsk and Luhansk (Conflict Armament Research 2021), pp.158–159, https://www.conflictarm.com/reports/weapons-of-the-war-in-ukraine/

46 Anon, 'Собственное оружие Донбасса', Topwar Ru website, 21 May 2018, https://topwar.ru/141808-sobstvennoe-oruzhie-donbassa.html

47 'РСЗО "Снежинка" производства ВПК ДНР. 13.06.2018, "Панорама"', YouTube, 14 June 2018, https://www.youtube.com/watch?v=VZcyOCQax2A

48 'РСЗО "Чебурашка". Вооружение производства ВПК ДНР. Эксклюзивный материал', YouTube, 3 June 2018, https://www.youtube.com/watch?v=5YqlUkTP23c

49 Various videos on the internet referring to a weapon called the 23mm *Separatist* rifle being fired in Donetsk appear to show a totally different weapon being fired from a tripod, possibly a single barrel from a ZU-23-2 adapted for tripod-mounted used as an anti-materiel weapon.

Chapter 10

1 Anon, 'В Донецке открыли музейную экспозицию, посвященную Героям ДНР', Ronin_077 Live Journal page, 19 April 2017, https://ronin-077.livejournal.com/53545.html

Chapter 11

1 Medvedev, *The Return of the Russian Leviathan*, pg.21.

ABOUT THE AUTHOR

Edward Crowther lived and worked in Ukraine for seven years from 2015 to 2022. He holds an MSc and BSc. This is his first work for Helion.